The Dead Presidents' Guide to Project Management

Essential Lessons for Project Managers and Sponsors

James Johnson

THE STANDISH GROUP

PLEASE RESPECT INTELLECTUAL RIGHTS!
Published by: The Standish Group International, Inc. 60 State Street, Suite 700 Boston, MA 02109 508-760-3600 www.standishgroup.com
This book is based on the CHAOS Knowledge Center
ISBN: 978-1-7335982-0-0
Printed in the United States of America

Acknowledgment

Thanks to Michael Johnson for the fine artwork of the graphic profiles of the presidents. Thanks to Jim Crear and Colleen Frye whose content contribution, advice, and patience in editing is commendable and highly valued. Thanks to Julie Sorensen for the both cover and inside book design. Thanks to all the Standish Group members who helped along the way. Thanks to the thousands of SURF members and CHAOS University attendees whose contributions made this work possible.

The president of the United States, when in office, is the most powerful person in the world. As of this writing, there are only 40 men, from George Washington to George H. W. Bush, who have held this esteemed office and who have gone to the great White House in the sky. Currently there are five presidents who are still above ground. It is important to note that most of these men were duly elected to the office by the majority of the citizens of the United States. Just getting to the office is a major accomplishment, and it took skill and perseverance to rise above their contemporaries to reach the zenith of all positions.

The Dead Presidents' Guide to Project Management considers 40 brief lessons that these great men have bestowed upon us. It is the author's opinion that the job of president of the United States requires a lot of the same strengths and characteristics needed by both project managers and executive sponsors. Most projects need both a strong, skilled executive sponsor and a project manager (or if an organization follows an agile methodology such as Scrum, then a Scrum master and product owner); and both positions can learn from our dead presidents.

The president of the United States must be a good project manager. Like a project manager, the president must use his or her domain knowledge, skills, tools, and techniques to manage and create activities in order to meet or exceed the expectations of the citizens of the United States. The president of the United States is a servant-leader, which means that he or she must have the skill to influence people to work enthusiastically toward goals identified as being for the common good. The president of the United States must also have good connections to be an effective leader. And he or she must be a good negotiator, with the ability to deliver bad news early and bravely, provide solutions, and be truthful.

Further, the president of the United States must be a good project sponsor, also called the executive sponsor. Like a good project sponsor, the president must inspire people. His or her enthusiasm must be infectious, so that it inspires the country to do great things. The project sponsor must be able to inspire, have an imagination, and have clarity of purpose. Clarity of purpose begins with a common understanding of the action needed to accomplish the vision. Finally, the president must be able to effectively distribute decision power, and understand the process of government and influence to get anything done.

My attempt in this book is to let the records of these 40 men tell the tale of leadership. Each of these chief executives provides a treasure trove of lessons learned and prime examples. These are not fictional characters. None of them are Superman. They are not faster than a speeding locomotive, nor can they leap over tall buildings. They are complex human beings. They are very talented, yet full of flaws. They are not all good men, but they all tried to do good things, and most of time the right things. It is often said that those who do not learn from history are doomed to repeat it. I would rephrase it to say those who can learn from history will be capable of improving on it.

In the words of presidential historian Arthur M. Schlesinger Jr., "The diverse drama of the presidency offers a fascinating set of tales." My hope for this book is that the set of tales presented helps to illuminate the rich lessons that these great men have brought to us. The diverse opportunities that confronted each of these presidents provide a backdrop into common issues facing project managers and executive sponsors on a daily basis. The major accomplishments and lessons of each president is exclusively the opinion of the author.

The Dead Presidents' Guide to Project Management

> "It is better to offer no excuse
> than a bad one."

George Washington

George Washington was the first president of the United States from 1789 to 1797. Washington had no formal education and his non-governmental occupation was a farmer and soldier. Before he held the office of president he was a member of the Virginia House of Burgesses and the Continental Congress. His major accomplishment prior to becoming president was leading the Continental Army to the conclusion of the Revolutionary War. He was also a primary force in the adoption of the United States Constitution. His major presidential accomplishment was organizing the executive and judicial branches of the United States government. Washington's lesson for project managers and executive sponsors is to learn from your failures and make improvements.

Many stories are told about the first president of the United States, including Washington's supposed statement: "Yes father, I did cut the cherry tree." Many have honored him for his truthfulness. However, Washington never cut the cherry tree, nor did he say those words. It was also reported that he threw a dollar across the Potomac River. But actually, Washington was much too cheap to throw money around. Many claim that Washington was a great general. However, in reality he lost more battles than he ever won.

Washington learned from his failures. He assessed his limited resources, found they were lacking, and formulated a strategy to overcome them. In The Standish Group's research report "Money Pit" we considered the true cost of a project in trying to prevent failures versus reducing these costs and having more failures. We compared this model project within two extreme environments: a mature institutional environment and a speculative agile environment. In the speculative agile environment a number of small projects failed. However, the educational value of their failures increased the value of the overall project program portfolio. In the mature institutional environment the program was completed, but it ended up having little value and was soon replaced.

The most productive inventor in history, Thomas Edison, also learned from his failures. He held almost 1,100 U.S. patents. Edison invented the phonograph – without him there would be no iTunes. Edison invented the motion picture camera – without him there would be no YouTube. He is best known for inventing the electric light bulb, which he did not. However, he did invent methods to make the light bulb affordable and long-lasting. Edison was a pioneer in both mass production of electricity and telecommunications. He once said the secret of his success was failing fast and inventing the affordable light bulb. He had 5,000 failures, plus one success.

What helped both Edison and Washington learn from failure was their attention to detail. Of all the skills Washington possessed, perhaps his greatest was in project management proficiency. He knew the details of his army's skills, tactics, strategies, supplies, and position. He also knew the details of the opposing army's skills, tactics, strategies, supplies, and position. Washington was a master of logistics and he would become the model for modern generals to follow.

Project managers are the custodians of details. Knowing the details helps the project manager learn from failures. Project managers can help the project sponsor learn from failure by reporting and analyzing the project details. Washington was a stickler for detail right up to the end of his life. On his deathbed he told his doctor, "I am going. Have me decently buried and do not let my body be put into the vault in less than three days after I am dead." In grief, the doctor nodded. But this was not good enough for Washington. He asked him if he understood. The doctor replied that he did. "'Tis well" were his last words. Washington made sure that the listener grasped his communications. Good communicators also make good project managers.

The Dead Presidents' Guide to Project Management

> "I must study politics and war
> that my sons may have liberty to
> study mathematics and philosophy."

John Adams

John Adams was the second president of the United States from 1797 to 1801. Adams graduated from Harvard College and his non-governmental occupation was a lawyer. Before he held the office of president he was a member of the Continental Congress, commissioner to France, foreign minister to the Netherlands and England, and vice president under George Washington. His major accomplishments prior to becoming president were the successful acquisition of funds for the Revolutionary War and the writing of the Massachusetts Constitution, which was the model for the U.S. Constitution. His significant presidential accomplishment was preventing a major conflict with France while improving trade and diplomatic relations with that country. Adams' lesson for project managers and executive sponsors is to be or find a good mentor.

Good mentoring can improve project success rates. In ancient mythology, Odysseus entrusted a mentor with the education of his son, Telemachus. The concept of mentoring has since been used to define a constructive relationship between individuals, with the purpose of providing support, guidance, and assistance to individuals in the achievement of their full potential. The role of the mentor encompasses friendly advisers, coaches, and teachers who are entrusted with the education and development of entire organizations. They possess advanced, or expert, knowledge in a particular field, and can expose organizations to new ideas and important trends in industry best practices.

Adams was a good mentor to two presidents. First was Thomas Jefferson, who became the third president. Adams guided Jefferson through the Continental Congress and the writing of the Declaration of Independence. Adams offered Jefferson concrete methodologies that he had used successfully in the past. Adams would meet with Jefferson during the writing of the Declaration, offering suggestions for improvements. Adams spearheaded the adoption of the Declaration of Independence with bold and forceful conviction, thus mentoring the timid and shy Jefferson by example. Adams would later help Jefferson establish himself as minister to France. Adams even provided financial advice and counsel to the extravagant Jefferson.

Second, Adams was a mentor to his son, John Quincy Adams. John Quincy Adams was a good protégé because he followed his father's advice. A good mentor must have the required fundamental expertise. John Adams was a good mentor because he had the required fundamental expertise as a diplomat and government executive. John Quincy Adams gained his presidential habits through mentoring by his father. Adams had his young son at his side as a delegate to France and Holland. John Adams was a good mentor because his experience addressed similar challenges, achieved similar objectives, and solved complex, system-wide problems that John Quincy Adams would face.

Knowing when to say yes or no is an essential element of project leadership, and a good mentor can help a project manager learn to say "No." John Adams taught Jefferson how to say it with boldness and forcefulness. Saying no is the hardest lesson for many project managers. Project managers must have the basic leadership skills necessary to direct and pilot the stakeholders and technical teams. Sometimes seemingly simple requests can put the project in real peril. Project managers need to assess each feature and function against business value, project quality, resources, risk, and the schedule. Senior project managers, like the senior Adams, can help new project managers, like Jefferson, by leading by example in establishing the areas of accountability, responsibility, and authenticity.

John Adams also helped John Quincy Adams to know when to say "Yes." Saying yes leads to project resources and brings those resources together. Project managers must have the ability to lead at the detail level – establishing what features and functions will be part of the project – and whether those features/functions are for the first phase, for a later version, or not at all. Changes that increase the scope and the time of the project greatly increase the chance of failure. A good mentor will help project managers learn when to say yes or no.

"I like the dreams of the future better than the history of the past."

Thomas Jefferson

Thomas Jefferson was the third president of the United States from 1801 to 1809. Jefferson graduated from the College of William and Mary and his non-governmental occupation was a lawyer and farmer. Before he held the office of president he was a member of both the Virginia House of Burgesses and the Continental Congress. He was also the governor of Virginia, minister to France, Washington's secretary of state, and vice president under John Adams. His significant accomplishment prior to becoming president was being the principal writer of the Declaration of Independence. His major presidential accomplishments included the purchase of the Louisiana Territory from France, and the executive support of the Lewis and Clark exploration of the Northwest. His lesson for project managers and executive sponsors is to find or make sure you have a good executive sponsor.

Executive sponsorship is when an executive or group of executives agree to provide both financial and emotional backing. In this regard, the executive or executives provide both the project's vision and the alignment to the business objectives. Executive sponsors encourage and assist in the successful completion of the project and ensure that needed resources are made available. The executive sponsor works closely with the project manager to set the priority for deliverables.

In Philadelphia on June 11, 1776, the fragile and uneasy Continental Congress appointed Benjamin Franklin, Roger Sherman, Robert R. Livingston, John Adams, and Thomas Jefferson to a committee to draft a Declaration of Independence. Franklin set himself up as the executive sponsor and then gave the task to Adams and Jefferson. Adams then left the writing to Jefferson. A draft of the Declaration of Independence was read to the Continental Congress. For several days members of the Continental Congress debated over each word in the Declaration and made their revisions. The 56 signers of the Declaration of Independence risked their fame, fortune, and their very existence by signing the document. Jefferson was able to accomplish his project because Franklin was a good executive sponsor.

In turn, Jefferson was a good executive sponsor for the Lewis and Clark expedition. He provided funding, inspiration, and vision to Captains Meriwether Lewis and William Clark as they set out on their famous expedition. He encouraged them to build a special craft to navigate the Mississippi and Missouri rivers. They had to overcome huge unexpected obstacles, but Jefferson's vision enabled them to keep pushing forward. Like Jefferson, a good executive sponsor has domain knowledge to add value to the project, and broad connections so when he or she needs support it will be there for the team.

Jefferson was an executive sponsor for his own projects as well. In 1768, he started building his home, Monticello, in Charlottesville, Virginia. In 1772, the base home was completed. Jefferson continued to make improvements until his appointment as U.S. representative to France. After his return from France in 1789, Jefferson began the modernization process to the iconic neoclassical architecture style. The home boasted many modern conveniences and innovations. Jefferson continued to make changes and additions through the rest of his life. These changes and additions were completed without interruption to his daily living and the operation of the family farm and estate. When Jefferson died in 1826 the home was still unfinished.

Jefferson was ahead of his time when building Monticello by using an iterative process and methodology. He built the Monticello baseline and then made ongoing improvements. Jefferson was not afraid to tear something down or out that did not work. He enforced change management so these changes did not stop him from using the home, and he would make corrections as issues surfaced. The real key to this approach was to develop new features in small, unobtrusive increments. Implementations that utilize this type of approach for adding new features and functions allow for better training and user acceptability, and satisfaction is much higher. Project teams should keep Monticello in mind.

The Dead Presidents' Guide to Project Management

> "Ambition must be made to counteract ambition."

James Madison

James Madison was the fourth president of the United States from 1809 to 1817. He graduated from Princeton University and his non-governmental occupation was a lawyer. Before he held the office of president he was a member of the Virginia Constitutional Convention, the Continental Congress, the Virginia Legislature, the U.S. Constitutional Convention, and the U.S. House of Representatives. He was also secretary of state under Thomas Jefferson. His significant accomplishment prior to becoming president was driving the adoption of the U.S. Constitution by the 13 colony states. Madison's major presidential accomplishment was the defeat of the British in the War of 1812. His lesson for project managers and executive sponsors is to be a good collaborator.

Madison collaborated with the Constitution's contributors and stakeholders. He found that doing so helped him to recognize weaknesses and tension points, determine priorities, as well as identify potential setbacks. Like a good project manager, Madison fostered collaboration. He found that stakeholders are more inclined to have a stronger commitment and sense of ownership if they feel their participation and contributions are valued. Through collaboration techniques project managers and executive sponsors can encourage input and feedback from stakeholders to create that sense of ownership.

Collaboration can provide answers to some very tough questions. For example, should the organization: Invest in this project? Hire more salespeople? Open a new plant? Develop a new product? Madison is considered the father of the Constitution. However, he was not the visionary; the visionaries were John Jay and Alexander Hamilton, who believed in a strong central government. He did not write the Constitution; most of the Articles of the Constitution were copied from the Massachusetts Constitution written by John Adams. In fact, Madison said, "The Constitution was not, like the fabled Goddess of Wisdom, the offspring of a single brain. It ought to be regarded as the work of many heads and many hands."

Madison was more like the project manager than an executive sponsor of the Constitution. Madison was a good project manager because he worked with his executive sponsors and developed a plan for ratification. He was a good project manager because he worked with his technical people and developed the formal legal documents. And he was a good project manager because he involved users, and through them developed the Bill of Rights to gain their support. The first of the original 13 states to ratify the U.S. Constitution was Delaware in 1787, and the last was Rhode Island in 1790.

The Constitution would not have been adopted by the 13 states if Madison did not have a rapport with each of their representatives and involve them in the project. This rapport included public and private meetings with citizens and representatives from each of the states. Madison was a good project manager because he had a strong bond with all of the Constitution's sponsors. The project manager can and should help the executive sponsor by generally connecting with the executive sponsor and creating a firm bond between them.

Collaborating and communicating with the executive sponsor is essential. A quality executive sponsor will have natural communication skills and use those natural skills to foster awareness and transparency. If the executive sponsor does not have this natural ability it is up to the project manager to fill in the gaps and provide the communication. A good executive sponsor will demand and a good project manager will respond with a communication platform that the executive sponsor can use easily. Together the project manager and executive sponsor will use the communication platform as a bully pulpit to advance the project's agenda. The project manager and executive sponsor will also use this platform to communicate with each other. Madison had such a platform.

The Dead Presidents' Guide to Project Management

> "A little flattery will support a man through great fatigue."

James Monroe

James Monroe was the fifth president of the United States from 1817 to 1825. Monroe graduated from the College of William and Mary and his non-governmental occupation was a lawyer. Before he held the office of president he was a member of the Continental Congress, minister to France and England, U.S. senator, governor of Virginia, and secretary of both State and War under James Madison. His significant accomplishment prior to becoming president was as an officer who fought bravely in the Revolutionary War. His major presidential accomplishment was the Monroe Doctrine, which declared the end of all foreign colonization in America. His lesson for project managers and executive sponsors is to gain emotional maturity.

Emotional maturity is the ability and capacity to perceive, assess, manage, and direct the emotions and actions of the project executive sponsor, project stakeholders, and project team. The Standish Group has identified 50 emotional maturity skills. These skills include the ability to recognize and deal with the Five Deadly Sins of project management, which are: overambition, arrogance, ignorance, abstinence, and fraudulence. Emotional maturity is also the ability to promote and institutionalize other skills such as community, honor, awareness, objectivity, and superiority. Emotionally mature people have the ability to deliver and deal with bad news, set expectations, and create and maintain fair rules of engagement.

Emotionally mature people know how to make decisions and make them stick. They also know how to gain consensus, and have effective collaboration and meaningful communication. On March 26, 1796, United States Ambassador to France James Monroe sent Secretary of State Timothy Pickering a report on France's reaction to the Jay's Treaty with Great Britain. The Jay's Treaty of 1796 was very favorable to Britain and unfavorable to France. The report was to contain three sections: Monroe's observations; France's formal statement; and Monroe's formal reply to France's statement. It should be noted that Pickering was a "dyed-in-the-wool" Federalist and Monroe was a Republican (later to change their name to Democrat).

The Federalists wanted a closer relationship with Britain and a more central monarchy-type government. The Republicans wanted a more populist type of government. When the dispatch arrived on Pickering's desk it only contained Monroe's observations and not the other two documents. Just before the dispatch left France, the French representative had requested a redraft of their response. Monroe also withdrew his formal reply without knowledge of the final French response. Pickering used this incomplete package as evidence that Monroe was incompetent and convinced President Washington to have him recalled. This was a major setback for Monroe.

Emotional maturity is the collection of basic behavior of how people work together. In any group, organization, or company it is both the sum of their skills and the weakest link that determine the level of emotional maturity. Monroe overcame his France setback and learned that emotional maturity is the key to success. Monroe learned to guard against ignorance from his Pickering encounter. As governor of Virginia he learned to set expectations, build consensus, and deal with arrogance. As secretary of state, Monroe learned how to overcome abstinence. Abstinence, in the context of project management, is the act or practice of refraining from participation and contribution to the project.

As secretary of war, Monroe learned how to set fair rules of engagement and deliver and deal with bad news. He also learned how to recognize and deal with fraudulence. Fraudulence can take many forms. In our book *The Public Execution of Miss Scarlet*, the title character does many things to try to cover up the real status of the project. Some of the things she does are intended to deceive her superiors and co-workers. As Monroe shows, emotional maturity can be improved, and when improved will increase project success. You can even become president.

The Dead Presidents' Guide to Project Management

> "If your actions inspire others to dream more,
> learn more, do more and become more, you are a leader."

John Quincy Adams

John Quincy Adams was the sixth president of the United States from 1825 to 1829. Adams graduated from Harvard College and his non-governmental occupation was a lawyer. Before he held the office of president he spent time in diplomatic missions to Denmark, Finland, Sweden, and Russia. The Massachusetts General Court elected him to the U.S. Senate. He served as secretary of state under James Monroe. His significant accomplishment prior to becoming president was being the first official U.S. representative to Russia. His major presidential accomplishment was improving the internal infrastructure of the nation. His lesson for project managers and executive sponsors is to create a project community for communication.

President Madison appointed John Quincy Adams as the first official U.S. representative to Russia. Madison provided Adams with a total operating budget of $9,000 per year. This included his salary, housing, and an entertainment allowance. To put this amount in perceptive, a St. Petersburg apartment for a diplomat generally cost $10,000 per year in 1809. The French ambassador's budget was $300,000 per year. Since Adams could not afford lavish balls and dinners he created his own informal community of parties that cost little to no money. These parties included

skating on the river, sledding down local hills, playing cards, and general exercise. A community in the context of a project, program, or ecosystem is a unit of a socio-political and economic organization consisting of a number of people, groups, departments, and divisions. Adams looked at his ecosystems and created programs that addressed the participants he wanted in his community. A community mirrors the informal organizational power structure and how work really flows through an organization. Adams set himself up as a permanent leader of his community, which had a casual and fluid structure. Participants came and left with changes in the diplomatic ranks. Membership and the power structure in a community are very dynamic.

While Czar Alexander I was the head of the community, information was the commodity of exchange and caused the community to be very dynamic. In fact, every morning Adams had a standing power walk along the banks of the Neva River with Czar Alexander I. This informal community gave Adams unprecedented access and influence, much more so than if he had used the normal diplomatic trappings. A healthy project community shares a common language, culture, and opportunity. A community can become a major part of the organization's communication platform. Adams' community over time replaced the court as the platform of communications.

Like Adams, you can build your own community by doing the following four things: 1) Assign someone to be the evangelist or spokesperson. It is always wise to pick someone who has a good reputation within the organization; 2) Make sure the executive sponsor understands his/her role as a champion in the community. He/she should always be noticeably visible and supportive; 3) Develop a common language that is easy to understand by everyone in the community. Provide a common means of demonstrating functions or features to your users; and 4) Get support to mandate to the community that everyone should board the train or get out of the station.

In Gary Hamel's book *What Matters Now: How to Win in a World of Relentless Change, Ferocious Competition, and Unstoppable Innovation* (Jossey-Bass, February 2012), he focuses on organizational management and the importance of self-directed teams and community. He also talks about a world in which transparency is a daily commodity because of the community of workers. The book provides a roadmap for building or changing a corporate culture to servant-leadership and turning the management pyramid upside down. It sends a warning signal that an organization must adapt and change to this type of management style or perish. Building an informal community around Czar Alexander I let Adams turn the management pyramid upside down.

The Dead Presidents' Guide to Project Management

"The people are the government."

Andrew Jackson

Andrew Jackson was the seventh president of the United States from 1829 to 1837. Jackson had no formal education and his non-governmental occupation was a soldier and lawyer. Before holding the office of president he was a member of the U.S. House of Representatives, a U.S. senator, a justice on the Tennessee Supreme Court, and governor of the Florida Territory. His significant accomplishment prior to becoming president was winning the Battle of New Orleans. His major presidential accomplishment was the establishment of the organized presidential campaign and current election process, which is based on citizen involvement. Jackson's lesson for project managers and executive sponsors is to gain an understanding of the users' needs.

In the 1824 presidential election Jackson won the popular vote, but neither he nor his rivals won the Electoral College majority. The election ended up in Congress and Congress selected John Quincy Adams. This procedure became known as the "corrupt bargain" since it did not follow the will of the people. Jackson then brought his campaign to the people. He focused on their needs and wants. He never lost sight that the presidency belonged to the people, not high-level government officials. He tuned in to the citizens' real concerns and understood that the people rule and promised to be a president who served them.

In the book *Tuned In: Uncover the Extraordinary Opportunities That Lead to Business Breakthroughs* (Wiley, June 2008), authors Craig Stull, Phil Myers, and David Meerman Scott present a compelling argument for focusing on real users' needs. Project managers and business analysts who are tuned in to the users' true needs will have greater success than those who just go through the process, no matter how good the process and procedures. While most of this book is focused on how to bring products to market that people will buy, for project managers it provides some very helpful hints on getting to users' true needs.

Stull, Myers, and Scott would point out that project managers might have an opinion about a feature or function, but they are not the users, so they would say, "Your opinion, while interesting, is irrelevant." Project sponsors and teams really want to focus on the true user needs. The project manager has to direct the sponsor and team to real users' needs. This was the power of Jackson. He was aware of the voters' needs, he understood them, and he concentrated on them. Jackson understood that the three elements of being tuned in to constituents are gaining empathy, looking outside in, and looking inside out.

If you want to understand your users like Jackson understood his voters you need to do four things: 1) Interview users to see if they can break down the requirements into different priorities; 2) Continue to ask questions. Who needs it? Why do they need it? What will be the value?; 3) Challenge the validity of the requirement; and 4) Keep a positive attitude throughout the process. Ensure your users that you are not attempting to hinder their process or work, rather you are attempting to help streamline it and make it easier for them. Finally, pick your battles carefully.

Jackson had empathy for the voters. He had the ability to understand voters' emotions and feelings. Jackson talked to the citizens to gain their consensus. He looked at their issues, hopes, and dreams from outside in and from inside out. Jackson looked at an issue from the outside by rating the citizens' feelings about the importance of the issue to the country. Then he looked at an issue from the inside by scaling their feelings about the importance of the issue to an individual. As a result, Jackson was overwhelmingly elected when he ran again in 1828. Jackson is considered the first president who was truly elected by the people and not the powerful elite.

The Dead Presidents' Guide to Project Management

"I tread in the footsteps of illustrious men."

Martin Van Buren

Martin Van Buren was the eighth president of the United States from 1837 to 1841. Van Buren graduated from Kinderhook Academy and his non-governmental occupation was a lawyer. Before he held the office of president he was a New York state senator, New York attorney-general, U.S. senator, governor of New York, secretary of state under Andrew Jackson, minister to England, and vice president under Andrew Jackson. His significant accomplishment prior to becoming president was the planning and execution to gain increasingly higher levels of government job stepping-stones to become president. In other words, Van Buren had no major presidential accomplishments. Van Buren's lesson for project managers and executive sponsors is to use stepping-stones to accomplish your goals.

A stepping-stone is a small but significant deliverable or an agile iteration. A stepping-stone activity allows for tangible inspection either visually or hands-on. Stepping-stones are easy because you can see them. Each stepping-stone is assigned an owner who is responsible and accountable for its completion. A project plan should comprise identifiable stepping-stones that are measurable, quantifiable, and concrete. Stepping-stones are key in the iterative software development process and lead to more deliverables or indicate the project is not on the right track.

Stepping-stones are powerful because they allow for rapid feedback, creation of feature velocity, and accelerated user training and acceptance.

Van Buren was no accidental president. He set out to become president and made it his life's ambition, and he used stepping-stones to achieve his goal. Van Buren had the greatest ability to adapt to the political situation of his time. Because of this agility his most popular nickname was the "Little Magician." He rose to the highest office with the adroitness of an NBA superstar going to the basket. In 1813, he was first elected to the New York State Senate. From this modest position, he moved from office to office, like crossing a narrow stream on flat stepping-stones, until he reached the ultimate goal as president of the United States.

It should be noted in presidential culture that during Van Buren's time, candidates did not directly campaign for, and were not usually present, during the nomination process. In order to be nominated, a candidate would have to act more like a reluctant bride than an aggressive suitor. In this Van Buren was a master, for he was nominated for president three more times. Van Buren focused on the needs of the delegates. Then he would assign an owner to a stepping-stone for a particular government project, monitor the results, and make sure that the owner accomplished the goal and carried his message.

If you want to use stepping-stones like Van Buren you need to do four things: 1) Establish your stepping-stones when you create your project baseline. Each stepping-stone must have a firm deliverable that your stakeholders can accept and use; 2) Hold meetings and education sessions with all project team members and stakeholders as to what the stepping-stones are and what is expected from each one. Continue the education process throughout the life of the project; 3) Assign an owner to each stepping-stone who is responsible for ensuring its success. At the close of each stepping-stone, have the owner present the results to the team; and 4) Maintain your stepping-stone baseline as a starting point along the way. If the end result of the stepping-stone is a feature that is not usable, or is rejected by the user, then you need to be able to get back to that earlier point. You then need to analyze what went wrong, correct it, and move forward with rework. Or in some cases, toss it out totally.

Van Buren always went back to his goal, which was to be the president of the United States. That was his baseline and he was never satisfied with less than being the commander in chief.

The Dead Presidents' Guide to Project Management

> "The only legitimate right to govern
> is an express grant of power from the governed."

William Henry Harrison

William Henry Harrison was the ninth president of the United States for one month in 1841. Harrison attended Hampden-Sydney College and his non-governmental occupation was a soldier. Before holding the office of president he was secretary of the Northwest Territory, territorial delegate to Congress, territorial governor of Indiana, U.S. congressman from Ohio, U.S. senator, and minister to Colombia. His significant accomplishment prior to becoming president was winning the Battle of Tippecanoe. Harrison had no major presidential accomplishment. However, he is credited with delivering the longest inaugural address. This address, delivered on an extremely cold winter day, is believed to be the cause of his death within 30 days of his presidency. Harrison's lesson for project managers and executive sponsors is that long, drawn-out communications, or too little communications, can both be project killers.

While Harrison is best known for the longest inaugural address and shortest presidency, one of the biggest reason he became president was the Battle of Tippecanoe. The Battle of Tippecanoe was fought on November 7, 1811, between the United States and the Tecumseh Confederation of American Indians. Governor William Henry Harrison of the Indiana Territory and his forces were camping by the Tippecanoe River. In the early morning while they were sleeping they were attacked by a group of the Tecumseh tribe. They regrouped and were able to win the battle.

The Battle of Tippecanoe cemented Harrison's legend and propelled him into his short stay at the White House. But note that Harrison had a poor communication platform – too little in the Battle of Tippecanoe and too much in his inaugural address. However, communication systems were hard then and it took days to get mail and other correspondence. In fact, President John Adams nominated Harrison to become governor of the Indiana Territory without informing him. Poor communications also led to an attack by the Tecumseh tribe. Project managers need to create a common and easy-to-use communication platform and verify that effective communication is in place.

Meetings are often used to communicate project activities. In his book *How to Run a Successful Meeting in Half the Time* (Simon & Schuster, June 1989), Milo O. Frank provides a primer on how to run a meeting. It covers the basic questions of why, what, how, where, when, and who of the meeting agenda. It illustrates methods of dealing with people and issues that increase meeting time and often lead to no conclusions. If Harrison had Milo Frank's book he might have cut his inaugural address in half and completed his presidential term. He might have accomplished great things.

Harrison would also have been better served if he had recurring communications. However, technology and habits of his time prevented such communications. That is no longer the case for today's project managers and executive sponsors. You need to make sure there are regular and recurring scheduled communications and meetings. The organization or the project team needs to adopt meeting standards that include meeting types such as: informational, problem solving, brainstorming, decision making, or a combination. The meeting should always have an agenda and objectives. People should leave the meeting with both a sense of accomplishment and what is expected from them in advancing the project.

Many of the agile methods have a standard on meetings, scheduled events, and communication methods. Even if you are not using agile, these communication tools could help you to have more successful projects. How to Run a Successful Meeting in Half the Time also contains a lot of common sense tools that are often forgotten about when running meetings, such as time limits, purpose, setting limited goals, and reducing participants. In addition, it talks about not inviting an important person through the use of a fairy tale. It only takes about an hour to read this book, but it will be one of the best hours you will spend. It is much more enlightening than Harrison's three-hour speech.

The Dead Presidents' Guide to Project Management

"I can never consent to being dictated to."

John Tyler

John Tyler was the 10th president of the United States from 1841 to 1845. Tyler graduated from the College of William and Mary and his non-governmental occupation was a lawyer. Before holding the office of president he was a member of the Virginia House of Delegates and the U.S. House of Representatives, a Virginia State legislator, governor of Virginia, U.S. senator, and vice president under William H. Harrison. Tyler had no major accomplishment before becoming president. However, he was a very active senator and congressman. His major presidential accomplishment was the annexation of Texas. Tyler's lesson for project managers and executive sponsors is to beware of conflicting visions.

Many projects have conflicting visions, and therefore lack a common goal. This is understandable given that there is the potential for as many viewpoints and reasons for supporting the project as there are stakeholders. This is especially true if these stakeholders are from many different departments and organizations. However, conflicting visions cause conflicts, and conflicts can cause the project to spiral out of control. The goal of the organization takes precedence over the goals of the individual or any individual department. Therefore, the project team needs to get everyone on the same page by testing the goal and reinforcing a common vision.

Tyler became president after the sudden death of President Harrison. Since he was the first vice president to experience turnover of the presidency he needed to establish himself as the legitimate office holder. He did that adroitly, but not without major opposition. Tyler had left the Democratic Party to join the Whigs and run for vice president. However, his politics aligned more with the Southern Democrats than the Northern Whigs. He refused to support the Whig platform and opposed many of their positions, including nationalism versus states' rights. His vision was in conflict with his supporters.

Tyler could have benefited from Dale Carnegie's book, *How To Win Friends and Influence People* (Simon & Schuster, 1961). The crux of this book is the principles for dealing with people so that they feel important and appreciated. These timeless principles are fundamental techniques for handling people: 1) ways to make people like you; 2) ways to help people come around to your way of thinking; and 3) ways to change people's minds without arousing resentment. Carnegie's fundamental techniques for working with people offer a guide for presenting your ideas while respecting other people's opinions and feelings. Project managers and executive sponsors can also benefit from this book.

Bill Coleman, venture capitalist, suggests leaders of any organization have the responsibility to adhere to the 3Vs: vision, value, and valuable. The leader must establish a compelling vision of why you are in business or why you are doing the project. The leader must prove why the project has differentiation and show how this differentiation has value to the customer. Then the leader must prove that the project is valuable to the organization and supports the vision. So the leader sets the vision, shows the customer value, and shows how that customer value is valuable to the organization.

A project's vision needs to be clear, concise, and comprehensible, but it also has to be the same for all the stakeholders. It is imperative that everyone be on the same page. Conflicting visions cause conflicts, and conflicts can cause complexity, which in turn causes confusion and drives up costs. Not too long after he became president most of the Harrison cabinet was gone and the Whigs threw him out of the party. In effect, he became a president without a party. This left Tyler without friends, connections, and very little understanding of the workings of his own government. Tyler also had no viable vision. He lost re-election.

The Dead Presidents' Guide to Project Management

"The Presidency is no bed of roses."

James Knox Polk

James K. Polk was the 11th president of the United States from 1845 to 1849. Polk graduated from the University of North Carolina and his non-governmental occupation was a lawyer. Before holding the office of president he was a member of the Tennessee House of Representatives, a member of the U.S. House of Representatives, speaker of the House, and governor of Tennessee. His significant accomplishment prior to becoming president was becoming a colonel in the Tennessee Militia. Polk's major presidential accomplishment was the Treaty of Guadalupe Hidalgo in 1848 with Mexico, giving the U.S. control over California, New Mexico, Arizona, Nevada, Utah, and parts of Colorado and Wyoming. Polk's lesson for project managers and executive sponsors is perspiration (aka hard work).

 Being a good project sponsor or manager is hard work and requires a commitment to the project or program. You need your own plan that describes this commitment and how much you will be involved with the project. The plan should include a communication method to get updates on ongoing activities and issue resolutions. A good project sponsor or manager can effectively champion only so many programs. You are a key person in the program. Programs are investments, and organizations need to get a return on their investments.

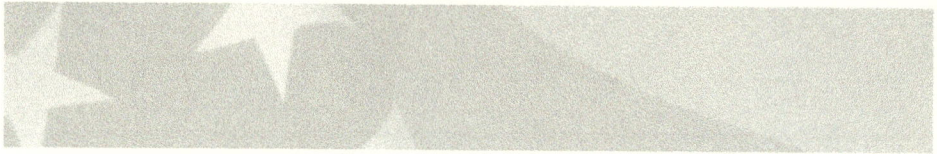

Many historians consider Polk as one of the top 10 great U.S. presidents. Prior to being elected, he pledged to be a one-term president, but would work harder and longer than any president, before or after him, during those four years. This workaholic president just might have accomplished that. Sadly, his reward for such a sacrifice was that he died less than four months after leaving office. However, during those four years Polk made the most dramatic changes in the map of the United States, as we know it today. Without Polk's hard work California, New Mexico, Arizona, Nevada, Utah, a good deal of Texas, and portions of Colorado and Wyoming might still be part of Mexico.

Polk set out early in his administration to either buy those Southwest Territories or take them away from Mexico by force. Polk saw the big picture, envisioning the United States from sea to sea. He set the agenda and ordered Zachary Taylor to use any excuse to invade Mexico. He worked hard to obtain funding from an uncooperative Congress to execute the war and was very clear on the objectives of the campaign. Polk encouraged his staff to provide full disclosure and minimize blindsides, have well-defined goals, and focus their hard work on objectives rather than procedural issues.

Today a common practice in many corporations is to have every employee, from the CEO to the entry-level clerk, define their business objectives for the year and make a commitment to work hard to achieve them. For example, these may include milestones linked to bonus money. The results are then measured against the committed objectives. The objectives roll down throughout the organization, starting at the executive level. Another thing is to have a crisp and clear 30-second elevator pitch. Polk used a similar process to make sure his staff was aligned with the big picture.

Polk often used metaphors to get his point across. He was a great storyteller and spoke in a way that created simple understanding. His stories added simple context for understanding the complexity of the endeavor. He knew that people have a tendency to listen and place themselves into the situation. Polk ignored his distracters and worked hard to stay on course. He forced Mexico into a treaty that included paying them $20 million for the Southwestern Territories. This was a real bargain. One year after the treaty, one of the richest gold discoveries was found in Northern California. Working hard can help your project teams strike gold.

The Dead Presidents' Guide to Project Management

> "I have no private purpose to accomplish … nothing to serve but my country."

Zachary Taylor

Zachary Taylor was the 12th president of the United States from 1849 to 1850. Taylor had no formal education and his non-governmental occupation was a soldier. Before holding the office of president Taylor held no governmental positions. His major accomplishment prior to becoming president was as a career soldier. Taylor spent 40 years in the army defending the United States in several major battles. Taylor was a significant force in both the War of 1812 and the Mexican-American War. His major presidential accomplishment was the signing of the Clayton-Bulwer Treaty with Britain, establishing that any Central American canal linking the Atlantic to the Pacific would be open to both British and American ships. Taylor's lesson for project managers and executive sponsors is to focus on the important items.

Often, project teams and sponsors waste a lot of time preparing for project checkpoints and status presentations and worrying about how the PowerPoint slides, which typically contain marginally useful information, look. The problem is, weeks go by, and facts change, and the business changes. Project managers should focus on the decisions and actions required to achieve the project goals. The team needs a few core metrics to ensure they are all aligned on progress and work ahead.

Taylor approached his duties with a laser-like focus. His battlefield accomplishments were many. In several battles he had fewer resources than his adversary's combatants, but he was able to focus on gaining the upper hand and pressing for victory. For example, in the Battle of Monterrey the city was considered impregnable, but it only took Taylor a three-day siege to capture it and send the Mexican Army into retreat. His helped his army understand and mitigate risks. He made sure they asked for help when needed. He would help them solve issues, and move the army forward. In other words, he did not waste time on unimportant busy work. Rather, he created a plan and ran with it.

One of the ways to optimize a project or portfolio of projects is to rate and rank them against each of the items for strategic goal focus. In a project you would want to compare each of the features and functions against the corporate goals or the goal of the project. The same goes for a portfolio where you would measure all of the projects against each other so that you can focus on the one closest to the corporate objectives. Like Taylor, focusing on the goals ensures that you are doing the right things for the organization.

To focus like Taylor you need to do four things: 1) Write on a whiteboard or flip chart the three main goals of the organization. In managing a portfolio write the three main goals of the project or projects; 2) Rate each project or feature using The Standish Group's five-point scale (see the OptiMix & CHAOS scales at the end of the book); 3) Balance to conform to a normal statistical curve, making sure you have a representative sample of the relationships. You need to measure all of the projects or features against each other.

During Taylor's short presidency, he was indifferent to most political issues and felt it was Congress' job to set the political agenda. Taylor believed his job was to administer the government and carry out functions of the established laws and regulations. Taylor ran the United States government like he ran his army. He used his cabinet members similarly to officers in the army. He had a single-minded view that Congress translated the will of the people and he would take his marching orders from Congress. Taylor felt he was a servant to the people through the collective congressional representation. He focused on the important items. Project managers should, too.

The Dead Presidents' Guide to Project Management

> "An exuberance of enterprise should cause some individuals to mistake change for progress."

Millard Fillmore

Millard Fillmore was the 13th president of the United States from 1850 to 1853. Fillmore had no formal education and his non-governmental occupation was a lawyer. Before holding the office of president he was a member of the New York State Assembly, a member of the U.S. House of Representatives, comptroller of New York, and vice president under Zachary Taylor. Fillmore's significant accomplishment prior to becoming president was his role in the anti-slavery movement. He had a major impact on the Compromise of 1850. His efforts in this regard made California a non-slave state. His major presidential accomplishment was dispatching Commodore Matthew C. Perry on a naval expedition to "open" Japan to trade. Fillmore's lesson for project managers and executive sponsors is giving and getting feedback.

Feedback is highly beneficial for preventing long-term waiting and wasted time. Executing lots of small projects will allow for rapid feedback. In order for feedback to be effective it must point at a particular feature, function, or action. Feedback only works if it is accepted. It also must be actionable and given with respect. If the recipient feels the feedback is not genuine, then chances are such feedback will be ignored. Finally, feedback must be timely.

In1850, Fillmore determined that Japan was very strategic to shipping. However, all attempts to open up the nation by the large European countries had failed, because at the time Japan was a closed nation run by a network of shoguns. Fillmore asked for and received feedback from his cabinet. His cabinet feedback was actionable, accepted, timely, and from a respected source. The cabinet feedback suggested that a show of force together with diplomacy would open up Japan. Fillmore sent an armada to Japan under Admiral Perry. Feedback helped the United States establish a new trading partner and the highway to the Orient.

Knowing how to give and receive feedback can make or break a project. In Michael J. Gelb's book *Work Like Da Vinci: Gaining the Creative Advantage in Your Business and Career* (Your Coach In A Box, April 2006), he presents what he believes are Da Vinci's seven principles: 1) Ask the right questions; 2) Put your answers to work; 3) Develop your business sense; 4) Turn uncertainty into opportunity; 5) Strike a profitable balance; 6) Integrate for success; and 7) Make the breakthrough connection. Rapid feedback is a very important part of any project and is especially important to the agile process.

If you want to get feedback like Fillmore did from his cabinet you need to do four things: 1) Get constant feedback; 2) Do not take any feedback, good or bad, lightly; 3) Promote and celebrate the positive feedback; and 4) Conduct surveys or focus groups before and during the project. Using this technique will give everyone a sense of satisfaction by knowing that they are being heard. Do a postmortem for feedback at the end to learn from your mistakes.

Despite asking for and receiving feedback from his cabinet on opening up Japan, Fillmore was not necessarily a good feedback role model. He was so closed-minded and uninspiring that in the 1852 presidential election the Whig party turned against him and nominated Wilfred Scott. During the next four years the Whig Party was torn apart by the slavery issue. One of the splinter groups was the anti-slavery American Party and nominated Fillmore for the presidency. The American Party was very secretive and it became known as the Know Nothing Party. When people would ask Fillmore about issues or to provide feedback his standard answer was, "I know nothing." In the 1856 presidential election Fillmore won one state with 22 percent of the vote. For the project sponsor and manager, feedback needs to be open and go both ways.

The Dead Presidents' Guide to Project Management

"Frequently the more trifling the subject, the more animated and protracted the discussion."

Franklin Pierce

Franklin Pierce was the 14th president of the United States from 1853 to 1857. Pierce graduated from Bowdoin College and his non-governmental occupation was a lawyer. Before holding the office of president Pierce served in the New Hampshire Legislature, and was a member of both the U.S. House of Representatives and U.S. Senate. Pierce had no significant accomplishments prior to becoming president. He was a brigadier general in the Mexican-American War, but fought without distinction. His major presidential accomplishment was the purchase of disputed territories from Mexico, which are now part of southern Arizona and New Mexico. Pierce's lesson for project managers and executive sponsors is achieving consensus.

Consensus helps create an agreement about the goals of the project. The project team should have a common definition of what success means in relationship to the project's resolution. Common ground is where the users agree to features, functions, and requirements. Common ground requirements may include things such as a database structure or a business process. Normally 80 percent of the requirements will be rooted in common ground. Some disagreement may come with the cost, schedule, or priority. There could be some disagreement on the creation and implementation issue, but generally common ground can be found.

The Democratic presidential convention of 1852 fielded many notable contenders of their time. The candidates included James Buchanan, Stephen A. Douglas, and Samuel Houston. Houston was projected to be the favorite earlier in the year, but as the field grew with high-profile entries and favorite sons his preconvention lead evaporated. He never even got close. In the first 16 ballots the contest was a three-horse race between Lewis Cass, Buchanan, and Douglas. In most of the ballots Cass would have the highest numbers and he came close on the 35th ballot with 131 votes, or 45 percent of the total votes. On the same ballot Franklin Pierce received only 15 votes, but that was 15 more votes than the 34th ballot.

The best way to gain consensus is through conversation. This is one of the hallmarks of a good project process. There is no tool, template, or guidebook that can replace the human aspect of a project or a presidential nomination. The Convention of 1852 was a team effort and required a consensual mode of adaptable thought, especially from the party team heads. Persistent interaction with the delegates brought about a consensus. The quality of work depends on the performance of the people.

Trade-offs and exclusions are good tools to gain consensus. Consensus is where each side or sides agree to give up something or include something if the other side does the same. Bargaining comes into play only with those items for which there is not clear common ground, only divergence of opinion. In the 1852 Convention the delegates had to first agree to exclude their favorite. The delegates then had to find an alternative candidate such as Franklin Pierce.

In the Convention of 1852 the votes went back and forth another 12 times. On the 48th ballot Cass was down to 72 votes and Pierce was up to 55 votes. Prior to the 49th vote, many of the states decided to meet privately to break the logjam. They first assigned tasks for delegates to interact with each other. They set up a standard protocol and small collaboration teams. First, everyone agreed that it had to be a fresh face and all of the notables would not be considered. Second, the candidate had to be acceptable to both the North and the South. On the 49th ballot Case and Douglas both received two votes and Buchanan none. Pierce received 282 votes, putting him over the top, and he became the Democratic candidate by consensus, and later the 14th president.

The Dead Presidents' Guide to Project Management

"The ballot box is the surest
arbiter of disputes among free men."

James Buchanan

James Buchanan was the 15th president of the United States from 1857 to
1861. Buchanan graduated from Dickinson College and his non-governmental
occupation was a lawyer. Before holding the office of president he was a member
of the Pennsylvania House of Representatives, a member of the U.S. House of
Representatives, minister to Russia, a U.S. senator, secretary of state, and minister
to England. Buchanan's significant accomplishment prior to becoming president
was negotiating a trade treaty with Russia. Buchanan had no major presidential
accomplishment. However, he did, through his many political connections, keep
an uneasy peace between anti-slavery and pro-slavery forces that kept the Union
together during his term. Once Abraham Lincoln was elected president his efforts
failed. Buchanan's lesson for project managers and executive sponsors is to have good
connection habits.

It is essential that both the project sponsor and manager be able to establish and
maintain connections to ensure a successful project outcome. Most of the people in
the project will be volunteers, which is the hardest group to lead because they have
no financial or security incentive to help with the project. Anyone who uses Linkedin
or Facebook has learned to make establishing and maintaining connections a habit.
Project sponsors and managers can use this newfound skill to the benefit of the
project.

Buchanan had a habit of creating and keeping connections. In a world devoid of all electronic communications Buchanan was a prolific networker. He would be constantly visiting friends, family, and businesspeople. He would show up at every occasion whether invited or not. He would follow up with notes to people he had just met. He would never say anything bad about anyone and would readily forgive people who harmed him.

In James Burke's book *Connections* (Little, Brown, 1978), he chronicles how one invention builds onto another invention that leads to more inventions. The three takeaways from this book are: 1) Without connections there can be no success or progress; 2) Success is a building process based on past work; and 3) Success is not an island and does not happen in a vacuum. Being a good project manager does not just mean knowing how to put schedules together, establishing procedures, and assigning the right resources at the right time. It also means knowing how to connect to those resources or team members no matter where they are located. It is finding the time to ask questions and having the skills to listen to the answers. True leadership is connecting to all stakeholders.

Buchanan was not a secretive man. He tried to keep communications open and honest, and he would never try to hide bad news. That does not suggest that Buchanan did not have strong beliefs, just his own way of dealing with them. For example, Buchanan believed that the states had a right to leave the union and used his connections to delay all-out war before Lincoln took office. Another example is that Buchanan, who was anti-slavery, would buy slaves in the South and set them free in the North without requiring or asking for reimbursement or compensation.

Buchanan's greatest talent was being able to see both sides. He was always soliciting suggestions, comments, and concerns from his large network. Because he had such a large network of influential people who both admired and respected him he could resolve many problems before they would become major concerns. He would remember the smallest detail about a person's family, life, and activities, and bring it up during their conversations. He would always address a person by name, with the most respect and courtesy. He said that the most important word in any language is a person's name. In sales schools they teach you to say a person's name three times during a two-minute conversation. In that regard, Buchanan was ahead of his time.

The Dead Presidents' Guide to Project Management

> "The best way to destroy an enemy is to make him a friend."

Abraham Lincoln

Abraham Lincoln was the 16th president of the United States from 1861 to 1865. Lincoln had no formal education and his non-governmental occupation was a lawyer. Before holding the office of president he was a member of the Illinois State Legislature and the U.S. House of Representatives. Lincoln's significant accomplishment prior to becoming president was an invention to liberate grounded boats. The patented product would inflate air chambers at the bottom of the vessel, thus raising it above the water surface. His major presidential accomplishment was managing the Union to victory in the American Civil War and abolishing slavery. Lincoln's lesson for project managers and executive sponsors is that less is often more.

On average, small projects deliver bigger value than large projects, which, on average, deliver small to no value. A small project has between six and eight team members, lasts no longer than six months, and costs no more than $1 million in normalized labor. Small projects have a higher than average value rating because the size constraint limits the functions and features to the most important and valuable. Large or larger projects often have medium- to low-value functions and features that water down the overall value because of increased costs and longer time to delivery.

A project's return of value only begins when users and stakeholders use the project's results productively. Small projects are 10 times more likely to be successful and return value than large projects. In addition, only about 20 percent of a project scope produces value and is generally used by stakeholders. In The Standish Group's CHAOS database, a collection of almost 50,000 projects and their details, we can clearly see that organizations that have a small project philosophy coupled with a high degree of failure tolerance have an exceedingly consistent high return of value. We also see that small, self-directed and self-reliant teams consistently produce projects with high customer satisfaction. A key ingredient to this formula is team members skilled in the agile methods and processes.

In the book *FIRE: Fast, Inexpensive, Restrained, and Elegant Methods Ignite Innovation* (Harper Business, 2014), author and Air Force Lt. Col. Dan Ward shows how small projects provide not only great value, but breakthroughs and disruptive innovations. In his book we learn to count only what counts. We learn about NASA's Faster, Better, Cheaper program and how it launches 16 programs for the cost of one. We also learn and consider the difference between complexity and easy, how to be more failure tolerant, and how taking more risk can lead to breakthroughs.

The Battle of Gettysburg began on July 1, 1863, around a town in south central Pennsylvania and ended three days later. When the battle was over the two armies had suffered between 46,000 and 51,000 casualties. The battlefield was then turned into Gettysburg National Cemetery in honor of the many dead countrymen and brothers. On November 19, 1863, there was a formal dedication, and the organizers invited one of the country's most well-known politicians to deliver the keynote address. On the day of the event this great orator bellowed his baritone prose for three hours, mesmerizing the awestruck gathered multitude.

The Gettysburg cemetery dedication organizers also asked another politician to say a few words and preside over the dedication. The lanky speaker rose and in a high and shrill voice spoke but a few words lasting less than 10 minutes. It was over so quickly most of the crowd didn't realize that he had spoken nor did they hear his words. Yet the world has long forgotten the words of the great Edward Everett, secretary of state, U.S. senator, and governor of Massachusetts. However, every American grade-school student must learn to recite that speech that begins, "Four score and seven years ago" by President Lincoln. Lincoln's Gettysburg Address is a clear lesson in "less is more."

The Dead Presidents' Guide to Project Management

"Washington, D.C., is 12 square miles bordered by reality."

Andrew Johnson

Andrew Johnson was the 17th president of the United States from 1865 to 1869. Johnson had no formal education and his non-governmental occupation was a tailor. Before holding the office of president he was a member of the Tennessee State Legislature, a member of the U.S. House of Representatives, governor of Tennessee, a U.S. senator, military governor of Tennessee, and vice president under Abraham Lincoln. Johnson's significant accomplishment prior to becoming president was managing the anti-Union forces and promoting the freeing of slaves in his home state of Tennessee. His major presidential accomplishment was the purchase of Alaska from Russia. Johnson's lesson for project managers and executive sponsors is to watch out for the toxic person.

Project managers and sponsors will often encounter team members who are exceptionally difficult to deal with, and teams are frequently forced to work with them under stressful conditions. Knowing how to manage a toxic person could be very influential to the success of a project. Project managers and sponsors may be tempted to do something rash to deal with the issue, but what they really need to do is talk things out. Project managers and sponsors should not let problems worsen because it is unpleasant to talk about concerns candidly.

Having the conversation with the toxic member is the starting point. Pull your difficult team member aside for a conversation. You do not have to be confrontational to be effective. Squarely address the specific actions that are having a damaging effect on the team, and ask for ideas on how to make things better for everyone. Spend some time in an informal setting, maybe over lunch, talking with your team about personal interests and goals. Every team usually has one member who gets along with the toxic person. Watch how he or she deals with your problem team member, and pattern your own behavior after his or hers. Encourage other team members to do the same.

President Johnson poisoned the congressional well when he vetoed the Civil Rights Act of 1866 that gave African-Americans equal rights. His veto outraged radical Republicans and united them with the more moderate factions of the House and Senate. Congress overrode Johnson's veto and it became law in April of1866. Johnson was committed to saving the Union, but he was also a southern slave owner. His views on bringing the southern states back into the United States were moderate to conservative, which caused much friction throughout his tenure as president. He was even at odds with members of his cabinet and other administration executives.

There are four things you can do to deal with a toxic person: 1) Figure out what works. Every team usually has one member who gets along with the toxic person. Watch how that person deals with your toxic person; 2) Take everyone out for a beer. Spend some time in an informal setting; 3) Redirect mean-spiritedness. If one person seems bent on creating trouble, try to find a new, more constructive target; and 4) Talk to the person, but quietly. Don't let problems fester because you're uncomfortable about openly discussing your concerns. If none of the above work then you must remove the toxic person to gain a more satisfying outcome.

In Johnson's case, he decided that he needed more allies in Congress, so he set out on a mid-term election tour he called "a swing around the circle." In the swing he would promote representatives who also believed in the moderate approach to Reconstruction. He would give speeches on his positions and defend his actions. However, he was not a good speaker. He could not control the hecklers in the crowds. He could not control his own temper and often lashed out at the hecklers, making matters worse. So another lesson for project managers and executive sponsors is that they need to make sure that they are not the toxic person.

The Dead Presidents' Guide to Project Management

> "My failures have been errors
> in judgment, not of intent."

Ulysses Simpson Grant

Ulysses S. Grant was the 18th president of the United States from 1869 to 1877. Grant graduated from West Point and his non-governmental occupation was a soldier. Before holding the office of president Grant had no governmental positions. Grant's significant accomplishment prior to becoming president was defeating the Confederate Army and ending the Civil War. Grant accomplished this major military feat against one of the great military generals, Robert E. Lee. Grant's major presidential accomplishment was signing the Civil Rights Act guaranteeing equal rights to African-Americans. He also enforced these laws and fought against southern violence against African-Americans. Grant's lesson for project managers and executive sponsors is failure tolerance.

Failure tolerance is taking on increased risk and allowing the project teams to fail without career damage and adverse reaction. The Standish Group suggests that project teams don't fail to fail. You cannot make real progress without risk. Taking risks will cause you to fail at times. The best hitters in baseball only get three hits out of 10 at bats. The only time you really fail is when you do not try at all. Failure tolerance is ingrained in venture capitalists who know that many projects will fail, but it is the projects that survive that are the real valuable ones.

Project managers and sponsors need to know that one of the ways to improve failure tolerance is the use of shared space. Ken Schwaber and Jeff Sutherland came up with the radical idea of shared space when they invented Scrum. With Scrum, the team is responsible for making the product work. The team self-manages without a lot of government and industry regulations. Small projects fit nicely into a shared space. Small projects support failure tolerance since they minimize the cost and time of failures. In other words, they fail better. Failing better is a key to succeeding better and creating higher project values.

On April 9, 1865, General Robert E. Lee surrendered the Army of Northern Virginia to Lt. General Ulysses S. Grant in the village of Appomattox Court House. The surrender ended the United States Civil War, after one of the bloodiest battles in the history of mankind. The terms of the surrender were very simple: Lee would turn over all large weapons such as arms, artillery, and public property. Officers could keep their side arms and horses. Each soldier could return home unharmed as long as they agreed and would sign a pledge not to take up arms against the government of the United States.

One of the reasons that Grant granted such benevolent terms to the failed Southern army was a speech given by President Lincoln six weeks earlier in which he said, "With malice to none and charity to all," referring to the treatment of the Southern rebels after the war. Lincoln wanted no repercussions or hostile responses to the Southern people. His vision was that the South would be respected and be allowed to come back as full members of the United States as soon as the war was over. Lincoln's assassination ended that vision. Andrew Johnson's administration was not in a forgiving mood and took their wrath out on the South. The underlying effects of those two events can be felt even today.

Grant did not win every battle, but was aggressive and took many risks. While it may seem orthogonal to good management and conventional thinking, high failure rates can be a good thing from a positive-value portfolio point of view. Positive-value portfolio is a group of projects that produce value for the investment. Many of the top 10 percent of companies that have the highest value rating have some of the lowest average success rates. These organizations have higher failure rates because they understand that it's necessary to risk failure in order to achieve exceptional success.

The Dead Presidents' Guide to Project Management

"The bold enterprises are
the successful ones."

Rutherford Birchard Hayes

Rutherford B. Hayes was the 19th president of the United States from 1877 to 1881. Hayes graduated from Kenyon College and Harvard Law School and his non-governmental occupation was a lawyer. Before holding the office of president he was a member of the U.S. House of Representatives and governor of Ohio. His significant accomplishment prior to becoming president was as brigadier general in the Union Army where he served with distinction and bravery. He was wounded several times in battle. Hayes' major presidential accomplishment was to implement civil service reforms by focusing on competence over party patronage in government appointments. Hayes' lesson for project managers and executive sponsors is trade-offs.

A trade-off is giving up some things to get agreement on other things. The race for the resources is measured by answers to some very tough questions. For example, should the organization invest in this project or should it hire more salespeople, open a new plant, or develop a new product? Consensus can occur when you can analyze, learn from, and build upon a combined knowledge base through stakeholder collaboration and feedback. In order to do this you need to create an open environment where honest mistakes or wild ideas are not penalized or criticized.

Trade-offs are all about negotiating. Herb Cohen's book *You Can Negotiate Anything* (Bantam Book, 1980) is a primer for learning how to negotiate. It underscores the basic skills that both executive sponsors and project managers need for negotiating. The three crucial elements to negotiating are laid out in easy-to-understand terms and examples. Many of the examples are more historical and some people may not be able to relate to them as well as others. However, the book is extremely useful to help understand human behavior in the act of negotiating.

In his book, Cohen tells us the three basic elements for negotiating are power, time, and information. These three elements together match very well against a project and the kinds of actions the executive sponsor, the project manager, and the stakeholders will need to negotiate. These negotiations will center around who can make what decisions, how much it will cost, how long it will take, and what information is needed to come to terms on an overall plan. Negotiating trade-offs requires giving up something to get something done. Sometimes that something is not equal and sometimes the power structure is not equal. Sometimes you have to settle for something versus nothing.

Here is a good example from the Hayes presidency on trade-offs and negotiating. Samuel Tilden won the popular vote, and he thought he won the Electoral College, so he believed he was the new president. However, there were 20 electoral votes in dispute. If they had gone to him he would have won by 19 votes; if they had gone to his Republican rival, Hayes, then he would have lost by one vote. So Tilden engaged in a bitter legal and political battle over who won the State of Florida. Tilden accused the Republicans of election fraud and ballot box stuffing. Tilden's supporters flocked to Florida to oversee the recounts and look at the condition of the ballots.

In the Hayes versus Tilden case a special board was set up to adjudicate disputed ballots. The controversy went on for months with no resolution. Congress had the final say on the election and it became a very partisan endeavor. In the end a backroom deal was struck: If the Federal government removed their troops from the South and ended Reconstruction, the Democrats would concede to the Republicans. Tilden lost to Hayes in the 1876 presidential election by one vote in a trade-off compromise. Sometimes trade-offs are really hard to accept, but they enable the project team to move forward just as the country did with Hayes.

The Dead Presidents' Guide to Project Management

"Ideas control the world."

James Abram Garfield

James A. Garfield was the 20th president of the United States for less than six months in 1881. During the Republican Presidential Convention of 1880, the Republicans had three popular candidates: former President Grant, James G. Blaine, and John Sherman. The first 33 ballots went back and forth with none of the three leading candidates getting a majority. The convention delegates then went to dark horse candidates. On the 36th ballot Garfield became the nominee and went on to become the 20th president. Garfield graduated from Williams College and his non-governmental occupation was a teacher. Before becoming president he was a member of the Ohio State Senate and the U.S. House of Representatives. Garfield had no major accomplishment before or after becoming president. Garfield's lesson for project managers and executive sponsors is to manage expectations.

Managing expectations is crucial. Remember the saying, "If you don't expect much, you will never be disappointed." The negative delta between reality and expectation is disappointment. Losing control of scope is often the first step on the road to projects that come in over budget, are late, do not meet specifications, or are canceled. Three ways to manage expectations are: 1) Don't overpromise; 2) Deliver more than expected; and 3) Deliver bad news quickly.

Garfield found out the hard way that managing expectations can be crucial. Charles Guiteau, a Garfield campaign worker and supporter, expected to have a prominent position in the Garfield administration because of his support during the presidential campaign. Garfield did not specifically promise Guiteau a position in his administration. However, patronage during this time was so widespread that since Guiteau was such a hardworking and outspoken supporter that he assumed that he would be given a job. In fact, there is some evidence that Guiteau never met Garfield. Managing expectations is not always just about explicit promises, but knowing what people expect. When Garfield did not offer him a job, Guiteau assassinated him.

In managing expectations you cannot just be proactive and reactive; rather, you must anticipate what people will expect. Often expectation is based on tradition and history. The Standish Group research shows that a small group of talented people is more likely to bring in a project with the appropriate functionality, on time, and on budget, because they can foresee expectations. On the other hand, large groups tend to use valuable resources in communication and deliberation without knowing what people are expecting. Many a project has run off the road and into the ditch because expectations weren't managed.

Garfield could have benefited from the book *Predictably Irrational: The Hidden Forces That Shape Our Decisions* (Harper, 2009) by Dan Ariely. Managing expectations is crucial to every project. The big takeaway from the book is the experiment on expectations. It shows how simple changes in the presentation can alter the entire way people view the product or service. It outlines how project managers and sponsors can use peer pressure to help drive the project – or sink the project if they're not careful. Another tool for the project manager is to use value and risk relative scores in presenting alternatives. The project manager or sponsor can show the value and risk comparisons to select the best options.

Speedy news is also essential to creating and maintaining expectations. If people are unaware or are misled about the progress of the project they will decide for themselves on the execution of the project. More often than not they will assume greater progress than what has been accomplished. It is up to the project manager and executive sponsor to set the expectations at the right level of delivery. In general, just recognizing that people often act irrationally and being able to identify that behavior when it happens is useful. In Garfield's environment he could neither set Guiteau's expectations nor recognize his irrational behavior.

The Dead Presidents' Guide to Project Management

"If it were not for the reporters,
I would tell you the truth."

Chester Alan Arthur

Chester A. Arthur was the 21st president of the United States from 1881 to 1885. Arthur graduated from Union College and his non-governmental occupation was a lawyer. As a lawyer, Arthur was out in front of civil rights by defending the rights of free African-Americans. He successfully defended runaway slaves. Arthur's significant accomplishment before becoming president was a suit he won against the Brooklyn Streetcar Company. The case is similar to the famous Rosa Parks case where an African-American woman refused to sit in the back section of the streetcar. After paying a settlement the Brooklyn Streetcar Company removed the segregation section. Before holding the office of president he was vice president under James Garfield. Arthur's major presidential accomplishment was modernizing the Navy through investment in executive sponsors and in steam-powered engines and steel hulls. Arthur's lesson for project managers and executive sponsors is abstinence.

Abstinence, in the context of project management, is the act or practice of refraining from participation and contribution to the project. Yogi Berra once said, "If the fans don't come out to the ball park, you can't stop them." If people on a project team have a choice, they may make the choice to stay away. If they have goals and commitments to their main jobs, and the project interferes with those goals, they will stay away.

Absence of critical stakeholders is the bane of a successful project. It is also a curse for the project manager and executive sponsor. It is up to the project team to assess whether or not chronic abstinence is a sign of more troubling problems and not just people being too busy. If the team believes lack of participation is not due to the normal day-to-day priorities, then the individuals must be addressed before moving forward with the project. Executive sponsors can also suffer from abstinence if they have too many projects to handle in addition to their day-to-day jobs. User, stakeholder, leadership, developer, and sponsor time is a constraint. This time constraint needs to be both understood and managed. People's absence and lack of participation is the downfall for many projects.

Arthur became an accidental president after the long and painful death of James Garfield at the hands of an assassin, leaving the vice president position vacant. Arthur chose Edwin Morgan to be his vice president, but Morgan refused. Arthur went ahead and submitted Morgan's name to the Senate for confirmation anyway. The Senate confirmed Morgan, but Morgan never showed up and the vice president's position remained absent throughout his term.

Finishing programs well is equally important to launching programs well. One of the mistakes many executive sponsors make is to get the initiative started, but not see it all the way through. Arthur was like a lot of executive sponsors who put in a lot of work up front to get the business case, the funding, and the program going. They then step back and let the project manager handle it the rest of the way. To add real value to a project requires time, so if an organization wants an executive sponsor who is more than a figurehead, the sponsor should not be overburdened with more projects that he or she has the time to devote to them.

Most of Arthur's presidency was uneventful. His major focus was on Republican Party infighting and patronage. Arthur was not nominated for re-election because he failed to deal with a budget surplus. Democrats wanted to use the surplus to lower import taxes, but his party wanted to keep high import taxes to maintain higher United States wages. James Blaine would get the Republican nomination, but lose to the Democratic nominee, Grover Cleveland. Arthur sat out the 1884 campaign. Blaine blamed Arthur for his failure because of Arthur's abstinence in the election.

The Dead Presidents' Guide to Project Management

"Honor lies in honest toil."

Grover Cleveland

Grover Cleveland was the 22nd and 24th president of the United States from 1885 to 1889 and from 1893 to 1897. Cleveland had no formal education and his non-governmental occupation was a lawyer. Before holding the office of president he was mayor of Buffalo, New York, and governor of New York. Cleveland is the only president to have personally executed a convicted criminal while serving as sheriff of Erie County, New York. Cleveland is also the only president to have two non-consecutive terms. His significant presidential accomplishment in his first term was creating the Interstate Commerce Commission to regulate shipping rates. His major presidential accomplishment in his second term was the use of federal troops to break up the Pullman strike. Cleveland's lesson for project sponsors and managers is to learn from projects that have failed, and to restart the viable ones based on that knowledge.

Over half of the successful and high-value projects are restarts when measured by either traditional or modern criteria. The Standish Group has six resolution measurements for success: onTime, onBudget, onTarget, onGoal, very satisfied, and very valuable. Meeting all six resolution attributes certainly could be defined as "perfection." In searching our CHAOS database of almost 50,000 projects, we found less than 500 perfect projects. This represents 1 percent of the projects from 2012 to 2016.

Digging deeper, we found that the one common trait of the 1 percent is that they were not "virgin" projects. Every one was a restart from a failed project. We would characterize most of the projects as simple, absorbent, fast, and economical. The majority of the 1 percent of projects were simple. Since all of the projects had failed once or more, the project teams learned how to deal with complexity. The organizations absorbed their lessons from the failed attempts and used this knowledge to create the perfect project.

The majority of the perfect projects were also fast. Almost all of the 1 percent were completed and delivered within six months or less. One reason that they were considered high value is because people could get some use out of the projects right away. Finally, the majority of the perfect projects had economical labor costs because they were small (completed with few people). You could count on one hand the number of perfect projects that we would consider large or had lots of people involved. Therefore, it is clear that in order to achieve more perfect projects they must be simple, absorbent, fast, and economical. .

Grover Cleveland was up for re-election in 1888. However, Benjamin Harrison defeated Cleveland on a high tariff issue. Harrison argued successfully that high tariffs protected domestic manufacturers. Harrison went on to pass the Tariff Act of 1890, raising tariffs. The unintended consequence was it made for higher consumer prices and the reduction of international trade. The tariff law became so unpopular with the voters that the Democrats swept the House of Representatives in the 1890 mid-term election. Cleveland, learning from his re-election loss, restarted his 1892 campaign with a promise to repeal the high tariff law. The same defining issue that defeated Cleveland in 1888 propelled him into his second term in 1892. Cleveland is the only former president to defeat a sitting president.

Cleveland was a man with principles and integrity. Likewise, the perfect projects had highly skilled project sponsors with integrity and principles. Like Cleveland, they inspired the stakeholders and the project team. Almost 80 percent of the 1 percent had a skilled team and a skilled project manager. Both the Cleveland administration and the 1 percent fostered a good culture, tolerated risk, and had a high degree of transparency. As Cleveland and our 1 percenters demonstrate, a knowledgeable restart can lead to success.

The Dead Presidents' Guide to Project Management

"The bud of victory is always in the truth."

Benjamin Harrison

Benjamin Harrison was the 23rd president of the United States from 1889 to 1893. Harrison graduated from Miami University of Ohio and his non-governmental occupation was a lawyer. Before holding the office of president he was a U.S. senator. Harrison's significant accomplishment prior to becoming president was as a Civil War hero serving as a brigadier one-star general. Harrison's Indiana Volunteers joined General Sherman in his march through Georgia. Harrison's major presidential accomplishment was the admission to the union of six new states: Idaho, Montana, North Dakota, South Dakota, Washington, and Wyoming. Harrison's lesson for project managers and executive sponsors is to use social media.

Executive sponsors and project managers should take advantage of social media products and concepts – microblogs, podcasts, vodcasts, wikis – to manage, collaborate, and communicate project information and activities. The Standish Group has long advocated that the three most important skills for successful projects are communication, communication, and communication. Adopting social media techniques and tools via platforms like Facebook, Twitter, and LinkedIn can provide for more effective communication. Social media can create a quality relationship with the users, stakeholders, and the project team. A familiar, easy, and straightforward method of communication is more apt to be used.

Harrison loved to talk and give speeches. He was also very good at it. He once gave 140 speeches all on different topics in a 30-day period. He loved big crowds and formal settings. He was the first president to attend a baseball game. On stage he seemed very friendly and relaxed. However, in person he was not very approachable and he preferred to keep his distance. In settings of small groups and one-on-one interaction he would tense up and become cold. He would become so frigid and formal that he became known as the "human iceberg."

Harrison would have benefited from social media. He could have exploited social media products and concepts to manage, collaborate, and communicate his presidential information and activities. They were, however, not available to him, but they are available to you. It's important for project managers and sponsors to create a social network and utilize collaboration technology to reach more people more quickly. A good resource for learning how project managers and sponsors can exploit social media techniques is the book *Social Media for Project Managers* (Project Management Institute, 2010). In her book, author Elizabeth Harrin explains how social media has improved the project environment and includes examples of using social media in the project process.

Social media can make even the most unsocial person more social by creating online habits. Social media levels the relationship game. Even a reclusive engineer can be on par socially with the most loquacious salesperson. Via Twitter you can post constant updates and feedback in small bites that can be easily digested by users and stakeholders. Via Facebook and LinkedIn you can also publish updates and make project friends.

In addition to public speaking, Harrison approached his work with a very formal method, resulting in an impressive set of new bills including: the McKinley Tariff Act, the Sherman Anti-Trust Act, and the Forest Reserve Act. Toward the end of his first and only term the economy went into a tailspin. His lack of personal sociability led to members inside the party to consider other candidates as their nominee as the presidential standard bearer. A weakened Harrison did prevail to get the nomination, but lost to Grover Cleveland mostly over the tariff bill in the only time a former president defeated a sitting president. While he was not personally sociable, in some ways you could say that Harrison is the father of social media. He was the first president to have his voice recorded. From this 36-second talk in 1889 he led all future presidents in electronic media.

The Dead Presidents' Guide to Project Management

> "Our differences are policies;
> our agreements, principles."

William McKinley

William McKinley was the 25th president of the United States from 1897 to 1901. McKinley attended Allegheny College and his non-governmental occupation was a lawyer. Before holding the office of president he was a member of the U.S. House of Representatives and governor of Ohio. McKinley's significant accomplishment prior to becoming president was the creation of collaboration methods to settle labor disputes. These methods are the foundation for modern arbitration programs. McKinley's major presidential accomplishment was the annex of Puerto Rico, Guam, and the Philippines as well as control of Cuba as a result of a settlement with Spain for winning the Spanish-American War. McKinley's lesson for project managers and executive sponsors is to have good decision habits.

Decisions need to flow for projects or a government to be successful. In a project there are thousands of decisions that have to be made during its life. In a presidential administration it could be millions. The Standish Group research shows that for every $1,000 in project cost, the organization will need to make 1.5 decisions. A $1 million project will produce 1,500 decisions, while a $5 million project will have 7,500 decisions. In order for the project team to successfully deal with the number of decisions the project manager and sponsor need a decision pipeline.

Latency between decisions is a major contributor to project delays and failures. Projects get behind a day at a time. They get behind because people cannot make decisions. Therefore, it is important to establish a process that enables you to quickly gain the decision information. Executive sponsors must ensure that their decisions meet the organization's strategy, and that the project team understands how all decisions tie back to the project vision. And project managers need to empower their teams to make timely decisions to keep the project moving forward and that are in line with the project vision.

McKinley had a habit of taking power by making rapid and firm decisions. In doing so he changed the face of the United States presidency forever, and today he is considered to be the first "imperial president." McKinley strengthened and broadened the power of the office of chief executive. His decisions on commerce, tariffs, and labor led to new prosperity after a national depression. He said while the Congress determines the objects and the sum of appropriations, the officials of the executive department are responsible for honest and faithful disbursement. He believed that decisions should be made to constantly care for the people's money.

McKinley made the decision that Cuba ought to be free and independent, and the government should be turned over to the Cuban people. After making the decision McKinley effectively directed the American military effort and the diplomacy that brought territorial acquisitions and peace. He used his office to direct senators and representatives to negotiate an independent Cuba and annex Guam, Philippines, and Puerto Rico. Thereby he managed the process and was the executive sponsor. He went to Congress after the fact to ratify treaties and confirm his decisions. As the project sponsor, he governed these new possessions through presidential commissions, similar to his own project managers or project office.

Not all of McKinley's decisions were wise, however. McKinley wore carnations all the time. He considered them good luck charms. On September 6, 1901, he went to the Pan-American Exposition in Buffalo, New York. A reception line formed and he greeted the people. In the line was a little girl. Charmed by the little girl, he decided to pull his carnation from his lapel and give it to her. In the crowd was an anarchist named Leon Frank Czolgosz. Within seconds of offering his carnation to the little girl, Czolgosz shot him. The crowd then jumped on Czolgosz and started to beat him. McKinley, mortally wounded, decided to yell to the crowd to not hurt him.

The Dead Presidents' Guide to Project Management

"It is hard to fail, but it is worse never to have tried to succeed."

Theodore Roosevelt

Theodore Roosevelt was the 26th president of the United States from 1901 to 1909. Roosevelt graduated from Harvard College and his non-governmental occupation was an author. Before holding the office of president he was police commissioner of New York City, a member of the New York State Assembly, a member of the Civil Service Commission, assistant secretary of the Navy, governor of New York, and vice president under William McKinley. Roosevelt's significant accomplishment prior to becoming president was reforming the New York City Police Department and reducing police corruption. His major presidential accomplishment was the building of the Panama Canal. Roosevelt's lesson for project managers and sponsors is to have a communication platform.

Roosevelt was a master at maintaining quality relationships. In order to maintain a quality relationship with the users, project managers and sponsors need to create a platform for communications. If the users and user groups have an easy and straightforward method of communication, the more apt they will be to use it. There are several ways to set up a user communication platform, and it has never been easier, cheaper, and quicker to do so. Channels are the means to communicate. Never before in the history of man have there been as many and as diverse communication channels.

A bully pulpit is an advantageous position from which to express one's views. It was Roosevelt's communication platform. Roosevelt called the White House his bully pulpit. He used this bully pulpit to bring the Panama Canal issue to the forefront. Roosevelt felt that the United States needed a canal from the Atlantic to the Pacific to increase commerce to Asia and other parts of the world. Digging the canal shortened the distance and vastly improved the movement of goods throughout America. Before the canal, ships would have to travel all the way around South America to get to the Pacific Ocean. Using his bully pulpit, he was able to get the Panama Canal project funded and passed through Congress.

A modern bully pulpit includes email, instant messages, texting, cell phones, conference calls, beepers, WebEx, video conferences, social media, and the old-fashioned way – in person. Yet with all these communications channels available, projects still fail because of poor communication, little or no collaboration, and lack of user involvement. Just recently a major British government project of a national database of sexual predators failed because the project manager and sponsor decided not to involve the users since they were too diverse and geographically scattered. They decided not to use their bully pulpit.

Getting the canal project passed and funded through Congress was just the start of Roosevelt's use of the bully pulpit. The Panama Canal was one of the greatest project management triumphs of all time. Construction on the canal began in 1904. The decade-long project was a massive undertaking. First, a railroad had to be built to haul equipment and material to the construction site. Second, terminals, wharves, coaling stations, dry docks, machine shops, and warehouses had to be built to support the construction. Third was the digging and construction of the canal itself. When Roosevelt left office in 1909, prior to the canal's completion in 1914, he used his bully pulpit to support the project through many of the most critical issues and events.

During the life of Roosevelt newspapers and books were the only mass media. Roosevelt wrote books on the armed forces, hunting, wilderness, American and English history, and many other subjects. In all, Roosevelt wrote 45 books. He also wrote hundreds of articles. Most of his articles centered on politics and his views of the current events. These articles would cause many more articles about him and his adventures, including his flight with the Wright Brothers, being shot then giving a 90-minute speech, national parks, and the teddy bear. Theodore Roosevelt not only wrote about history, he made it.

"Don't write so that you can be understood, write so that you can't be misunderstood."

William Howard Taft

William Taft was the 27th president of the United States from 1909 to 1913. Taft graduated from Yale College and Cincinnati Law School and his non-governmental occupation was a lawyer. Before holding the office of president he was an Ohio Superior Court judge, U.S. solicitor general, U.S. Circuit Court judge, governor of the Philippines, and secretary of war under Theodore Roosevelt. His significant accomplishment prior to becoming president was establishing a democracy in the Philippines and drafting their constitution, similar to the U.S. Constitution. Taft's major presidential accomplishment was the passage of the 16th Amendment codifying the federal government's authority to tax income without apportioning it among the states. Taft's lesson for project managers and executive sponsors is that the executive sponsor should be visible.

Taft himself was visible. During his presidency he weighed 330 pounds and stood 6 feet tall. A visible sponsor who really knows what the team is doing means a whole lot more than someone who just flies in and says someone is doing a good job. The project team needs to know the sponsor knows what they are doing. A visible and collaborative executive sponsor knows who is contributing. The project sponsor or manager can touch the finished product and provide real perception on the contributions. The project sponsor should be, from that perspective, visible to the team.

A good example of visibility comes from Gloria Cordes Larson, president of Bentley University. Larson considers the executive sponsor role an integral part of her normal job. When she became president of Bentley, she decided that she would try to be both visible and accessible. She attended numerous meetings and functions on and off campus every week. She would have parties at her home for students, faculty, staff, trustees, and alumni throughout the year. She took every chance she could to talk about the school's plans and get feedback. She believes a sponsor should always be on the lookout for opportunities to help the team get more support.

Taft approached his work in a similar way. President McKinley appointed Taft as Governor General of the Philippines with a mission to set up a civil government. Taft first removed the military commander and reduced hostilities. He improved the overall economy and set up home ownership through low-cost loans. He worked with local politicians to set up a system of self-rule. Taft soon became the face of the Philippines. Filipino residents loved Taft because they saw visibly that he supported them and made their life better. It would take over 40 years for the Philippines to gain independence, but the process was started by Taft's vision and visibility.

Visibility in general improves the success and value of any project. It is not only the responsibility of the project sponsor and manager, but the project team as well. The team's work has to be visible. This requires that the team be visible about what they have accomplished and what they need to accomplish.

In Taft's case, he loved baseball and enjoyed going to major league games. In 1910, Taft created a tradition by throwing out the first pitch on opening day. He is also responsible for another tradition. It is customary that people in the presence of the chief executive of the United States stand when the president stands. Because of his size Taft often needed to get up and move around. During his trips to the ballpark he would often get up in the middle of the seventh inning and stretch. Since he was so large, everyone was aware when he stood up and they too had to stand. Today, if you go to any major league baseball game during the middle of the seventh inning the crowd will get up and do the "7th Inning Stretch." The legacy of his lesson for executive sponsors is to stand tall and wide. At Fenway Park during the 7th Inning Stretch the Red Sox crowd will sing "Sweet Caroline," and it is so good.

The Dead Presidents' Guide to Project Management

> "The man who is swimming against the stream knows the strength of it."

Woodrow Wilson

Woodrow Wilson was the 28th president of the United States from 1913 to 1921. Wilson graduated from Princeton University and his non-governmental occupation was a teacher. Before holding the office of president he was governor of New Jersey. His significant accomplishment prior to becoming president was initiating reforms at Princeton University as their president. His major presidential accomplishment was winning the Nobel Prize for all his achievements in office. One of his presidential accomplishments was the passing of the 19th Amendment to the U.S. Constitution, which guaranteed American women the right to vote. Another was the creation of the Federal Reserve Bank to make the U.S. banking system more responsive to national economic conditions. Wilson's lesson for project managers and project sponsors is to iterate.

The Standish Group research shows that some of the most valuable projects are those that have failed and then get restarted. The iterative process within the agile methodology is the cornerstone of all the different methodologies. The iterative process is a trial-and-error approach. Teams try something out to see what works and what does not work, improve on it, and then try again. Constant iteration improves general quality and usability. One of the most important benefits of iteration is the discovery of design flaws that show up very quickly.

In John Maxwell's book *Failing Forward, Turning Mistakes into Stepping Stones for Success* (Thomas Nelson, March 2000), he provides several steps for failing forward. Some examples are: 1) Realize there is one major difference between average and achieving people; 2) Learn a definition of failure; 3) Remove the "you" from failure; and 4) Work on the weakness that weakens you. Many people are afraid of failure. It is Standish Group's strong belief that you can only be successful after you have failed. Maxwell's book has great insight about how to embrace and learn from failure using iteration.

The League of Nations (League) was the brainchild of Woodrow Wilson. It was established after World War I to help prevent future wars. The League had a set of rules to manage disputes through collaboration and communication. While its main purpose was to prevent future wars, the League also supervised labor conditions; global health; and protection of minorities, minors, and prisoners of war. The League operated out of Geneva, Switzerland, until 1945. However, it failed to achieve its goal of preventing World War II. And while at its height the League had 58 country members, the United States was not one of them. Wilson failed to get ratification from the United States Senate, but it did not stop him from iterating.

Kent Beck, one of the founders of the agile movement, suggests using conversation as a best practice for software development. There is constant dialogue between business and technology. Requirements or specifications are put down on 3X5 or 5X8 inch index cards. The collection of cards is a story, with each card being one part of the story. The agile iterative process starts with the story.

Wilson toured the United States countryside using conversations to try to get support for the League. However, the United States was not ready to become the world's policeman or be part of a global police force. The failure of the United States to join the League sealed its fate, but most likely it was indecision and the inability of members to come to a unified agreement that caused the downfall. The purpose of preventing wars was a noble and good cause; however, expanding the charter to other areas broadened the League's focus and led to other minor conflicts among the nations. The League's inability to enforce its own rules and sanctions proved it had little value on the world stage. The most significant outcome from the League was its reincarnation as The United Nations. The lesson to project sponsors and managers is the United Nations is an iterative product of the League.

The Dead Presidents' Guide to Project Management

> "Treat your friend as if he will one day be your enemy, and your enemy as if he will one day be your friend."

Warren Gamaliel Harding

Warren G. Harding was the 29th president of the United States from 1921 to 1923. Harding graduated from Ohio Central College and his non-governmental occupation was an editor and publisher. Before holding the office of president he was an Ohio state senator, lieutenant-governor of Ohio, and U.S. senator. His significant accomplishment prior to becoming president was the financial turnaround of the local newspaper. Through his newspaper, Harding established himself as a fair and magnanimous provider of truth, justice, and the American way. His major presidential accomplishment was establishment of the Veterans Bureau to handle veterans' medical and job needs. Harding's lesson for project managers and executive sponsors is to watch out for the project saboteur.

Almost every project will create winners and losers. Some people will gain power and some will lose it. The first thing you need to do is identify those people who will lose power – these are your potential project saboteurs. Next, you need to recognize the project saboteurs. In their book *The Project Saboteur* (Claret Press, May 2016), Dion Kotteman and Jeroen Gietema help you identify the habits and behaviors of a potential saboteur. Knowing who they are enables you to neutralize their effectiveness. Kotteman and Gietema also give you the tools to help deal with the potential saboteurs.

Often projects fail not because of the actions of people, but their inactions. This passive-aggressive approach is often used successfully by project saboteurs. Project stakeholders must be active participants, not passive customers. Project saboteurs, as stakeholders, rightfully can demand the authority to approve project deliverables, either wholly or in part. As we've said many times, "Time is the enemy of all projects." Therefore, untimely decisions and delays are a project saboteur's best weapon. Having a decision process or pipeline helps to move things along and can mitigate damage done by a project saboteur.

An example is a project that for confidentiality reasons we'll call Project Goldfish. It got officially underway with the project sponsor, the VP of Finance, giving a motivational speech and luncheon for the team. There were several key stakeholders and most of them did not report to the VP of Finance, but were peers. There were several areas where the new project would reduce head count, budget, power, and prestige from the other executives. One executive insisted on a set of features that doubled the project scope. Another executive sent junior people to user meetings, claiming time pressure. Yet another would not make timely decisions, claiming lack of information and data. There was no outright rebellion. It was just a lack of interest that caused the project to be canceled.

Increasing decision latency, which is the time between issue discovery and resolution, is a favorite strategy for project saboteurs. This is especially true in the early stages of the project where a project saboteur is needed in helping to define deliverables, provide complete, timely reviews of interim deliverables, and expedite the project manager's access to subject matter expertise. Sometimes the project saboteur could be a friend of the project.

This gets us back to Harding. The Teapot Dome was a scandal involving Harding's Secretary of the Interior Albert Fall. Fall did a secret leasing deal for federal oil reserves and got kickbacks from Sinclair Oil. Harding was never tied to the crime other than two major decisions, one appointing Fall to his cabinet, and the other moving the oil rights from the Department of the Navy to Interior. However, Harding was slow to take action and let Congress do most of the investigation, which ultimately led to Fall's conviction. Fall was the saboteur, but he was not recognized. In response to the scandal, Harding is reported to have made these immortal remarks: "I have no trouble with my enemies, but my damn friends, they're the ones that keep me walking the floor nights!"

> "It takes a great man
> to be a good listener."

Calvin Coolidge

Calvin Coolidge was the 30th president of the United States from 1923 to 1929. Coolidge graduated from Amherst College and his non-governmental occupation was a lawyer. Before holding the office of president he was a member of the Massachusetts Legislature; mayor of Northampton, Massachusetts; lieutenant-governor of Massachusetts; governor of Massachusetts; and vice president under Warren Harding. His significant accomplishment prior to becoming president was the breakup of the Boston Police work stoppage. He called out the state's National Guard and declared that public safety does not go on strike anytime, anywhere. Coolidge's major presidential accomplishment was the establishment of the Federal Communications Commission (FCC). Coolidge's lesson for project managers and executive sponsors is to be a good listener.

Both project sponsors and managers need to develop attentive listening skills. Attentive listening is more than just hearing someone's words; it is understanding their body language, facial expressions, and demeanor. Look for the person's tone of voice or body language for hints as to how they feel about getting involved in the project. The project team can use this information in their interaction and to move the project forward. Attentive listening provides encouragement and makes people feel important. It is also one of the most difficult communication skills. However, project managers and sponsors need to acquire and maintain this skill in order to improve project outcomes.

Listening is a learned skill and habit that takes practice and concrete feedback. To get better at being a good listener you might try using a technique known as reflective listening. Reflective listening is hearing someone speak, rephrasing what they said without judgment or commentary, and then asking the person to confirm your understanding. For example, a speaker says, "The dog is pink." The listener's natural reply would be to say, "No, the dog is white," since it is white. Instead, you should say, "I understand you think the dog is pink," and ask if that is correct. The speaker might say that the listener understood him. Later in the conversation you might be able to introduce the fact that the dog is white, because you earned the speaker's trust that you heard him.

Good listening is a key tool to discover and uncover both project saboteurs and supporters. Just think how much better you could do with stubborn stakeholders, users, and project team members. Coolidge once said, "No man ever listened himself out of a job," and "It takes a great man to be a good listener." It is obvious that good judgment starts with good listening. The rule of thumb is to listen twice as much as you speak.

You have to be a good listener to build effective relationships, but we all know that it's not as easy as it looks. Proficient communicators try to listen generously – with a deep appreciation for the speaker's feelings, reality, and commitment. Good listening is a highly effective tool that helps you solve emotionally charged problems and resolve interpersonal conflicts. It contributes to creative collaboration, faster decision making, easier sharing of resources, and general job satisfaction. Good listening shifts the emphasis from right and wrong to compromise and collaboration. Don't jump to conclusions. You cannot assume that what you are hearing is identical to what the speaker intended to communicate.

Listening is not a passive activity. How you listen helps shape the conversation and the speaker's thinking. However, don't let your enthusiasm carry you into a debate. Refrain from arguing about facts. Ask only questions that assist you in understanding the speaker's perspective. What you think is less relevant than what you hear. Coolidge's dry Yankee wit and frugality with words is legendary. Yet Coolidge's words are some of the most quoted words by other presidents who followed him. Coolidge was a great believer in less is more, and perfected the art of using a few powerful words to achieve greatness.

The Dead Presidents' Guide to Project Management

> "Wisdom consists not so much in knowing what to do in the ultimate as knowing what to do next."

Herbert Clark Hoover

Herbert Hoover was the 31st president of the United States from 1929 to 1933. Hoover graduated from Stanford University and his non-governmental occupation was an engineer. Before holding the office of president he was secretary of commerce under both Warren Harding and Calvin Coolidge. His significant accomplishment prior to becoming president was as the head and the driving force of the American Relief Administration, which helped post-World War I Europe feed its people. Hoover's efforts saved millions of people. Hoover was president during the Great Depression. His major presidential accomplishment was the building of the Hoover Dam. Hoover's lesson for project managers and executive sponsors is to work with the right process.

Not all methods work for all organizations or projects. There are many methodologies, but they boil down to three broad categories: agile, waterfall, and other. Agile is currently a growing choice. For the first time in 20 years, agile projects outnumber waterfall projects in The Standish Group's CHAOS database. Agile projects use self-directed teams and an iterative style. Waterfall projects break up the process into steps, each of which must be completed before moving to the next. "Other" can be a combination of agile and waterfall, or a totally different approach. The right process can make the difference between success and failure.

Once a process is established, Standish suggests that executives and project teams follow the established process and not divert from it. The organization should lay the development process from end to end that works for them. The project team normally knows what they are supposed to do and are ready and willing to do it. However, when the executive sponsor changes the established process and diverts the team it generally creates more work, delays, and cost overruns. Predictability is the important benefit of a process. The organization needs to know when and what will be delivered so it can put plans in place to take advantage of the work product. In many cases the entire company might be organized around a new product. If the product is late or deficient it could put the company in jeopardy.

A lean process improves success and value. A lean process has few moving parts, and those parts are automated and streamlined. Projects flow through the system like a pipeline. Lean execution does not mean there is no governance; it just means that governance is a framework that allows teams broad latitude within the organizational environment. Lean execution does not mean there is no compliance; it just means that compliance is results oriented versus reporting oriented. Lean execution still has key performance indicators (KPIs), but just a few very important KPIs. And project management tools are used sparingly, with only a few features.

Hoover knew how to utilize process to get things done. When most people think of Hoover, they normally think of his inactions during the Great Depression. However, in Belgium they have a different view of this engineer-turned-politician. Leuven, Belgium, named a high-traffic square after Hoover for his work in helping to feed their citizens after Belgium was invaded by Germany in World War I.

Hoover took over the operation of the Committee for Relief in Belgium (CRB) and made it a highly efficient organization, delivering millions of tons of food to millions of starving citizens. Working from London, he would travel to Belgium and meet with German officials and get them to allow the incoming food shipments. Hoover later would adapt his methods and processes to other relief efforts and projects. Unfortunately, his efforts to adapt his methods to the U.S. government did not meet with success. As organizations adapt different types of methods they need to think about Hoover. On the other hand, he did get his dam built.

"The only thing we have
to fear is fear itself."

Franklin Delano Roosevelt

Franklin Roosevelt was the 32nd president of the United States from 1933 to 1945. Roosevelt graduated from Harvard College and his non-governmental occupation was a lawyer. Before holding the office of president he was a member of the New York State Legislature, assistant secretary of the Navy, and governor of New York. His major accomplishment prior to becoming president was his command of the Navy's Aviation Division in World War I. Roosevelt had many major presidential accomplishments including the New Deal, thus ending the Great Depression; ending Prohibition; and the creation of the Federal Deposit Insurance Corporation (FDIC). Roosevelt's lesson for project managers and sponsors is the Theory of Constraints.

Constraints theory comprises three broad concepts: artificial constraints, real constraints, and realistic constraints. Constraints are limitations or restrictions, and are very important attributes in defining a project or program. A project simply cannot exist without constraints. Constraints can work to mitigate or aggravate the law of diminishing returns. The Standish Group has identified several constraints that we use to measure and optimize projects: money, time, timing, scope, capability, resources, complexity, risk, goal, and order. There are other constraints that we do not measure, such as process, compliance, governance, procedure, and emotion. When Roosevelt took office he had all constraint types working against him: artificial, real, and realistic.

In his first inaugural address, Roosevelt said, "Our distress comes from no failure of substance. We are stricken by no plague of locusts. Compared with the perils which our forefathers conquered because they believed and were not afraid ..." Roosevelt is saying that failure is our own lack of confidence, brought about by ourselves, not by outside forces. This was his artificial constraint. It is important to reduce the effects of artificial constraints to improve project value and increase customer satisfaction. Many of these artificial constraints are unnecessary to manage the project, and often prevent users and sponsors from reaching a compromise and planning a course of action.

Real constraints are money, time, scope, and capability. Money is a key constraint. The right amount of money will support the project; too much money undermines it. Eliyahu Goldratt's *Beyond the Goal* (Your Coach in a Box, 2005) outlines the theory of constraints in a simple, useful, and practical manner. The book also provides insight into how a constraint can prevent the project from achieving its goal. In *The Phoenix Project* (IT Revolution Press, 2014), authors Gene Kim, Kevin Behr, and George Spafford use Goldratt's constraints to eliminate artificial and real constraints from their IT DevOps. Solving these constraints saves the company.

When Roosevelt took office the country was in the middle of the Great Depression (real constraints). A quarter of the workers in the United States were unemployed. Anything Roosevelt did would be both risky and complex. Realistic constraints are risky and complex, just like all projects are risky and naturally complex. Roosevelt assessed his options and created the New Deal. Your organization has the option to optimize project risk by starting with a risk assessment. However, there is good risk and bad risk. Good risk is taking chances that can lead to true breakthroughs. Bad risk is doing things that you know do not work. Roosevelt's New Deal was a true breakthrough.

T. S. Eliot said, "Only those who will risk going too far can possibly find out how far one can go." Too much of the project management profession has centered on eliminating and managing risk. Taking risk is the only way to move forward, but take smart risks and allow for failure. The 18th Amendment of the U.S. Constitution effectively established the prohibition of alcoholic beverages by declaring the production, transport, and sale of alcohol to be illegal. One of the best things Roosevelt did was end Prohibition, thus making all risky behavior less restrained.

The Dead Presidents' Guide to Project Management

> "It is amazing what you can accomplish
> if you do not care who gets the credit."

Harry S. Truman

Harry S. Truman was the 33rd president of the United States from 1945 to 1953. Truman attended the University of Kansas City Law School and his non-governmental occupation was a farmer and store owner. Before holding the office of president he was a county judge, U.S. senator, and vice president under Franklin Roosevelt. His significant accomplishment prior to becoming president was uncovering and stopping wasteful defense spending. His major presidential accomplishment was forcing the Japanese surrender in World War II. He also guided the American economy through a post-war recession and started the racial integration of the military. Truman's lesson for project managers and executive sponsors is to take passionate ownership.

A passionate owner or project sponsor is a must for a successful project. Projects typically must be sold and resold. There are times when the project manager must help the executive sponsor to function as a salesperson to maintain the commitment of stakeholders and the sponsor's peers. With project plans in hand, project managers with the help of the executive sponsor may need to periodically remind people about the business need that is being met and that their contributions are essential to help meet this need. Project success is correlated with true business need for project deliverables.

Truman had a habit of taking passionate ownership of a problem. He had a small sign on his deck that said "The buck stops here," meaning he was willing to take the ultimate responsibility or ownership for the decisions of his administration. One of his most famous lines was: "A pessimist is one who makes difficulties of his opportunities and an optimist is one who makes opportunities of his difficulties." Truman was a fighter and he would carry the solution to Congress. He would not let them bring the solution to him. He would own the problem and solution. Truman thought it was important to foster the sense of pride and accomplishment that comes with ownership of any issue important to a project.

Commitment is stronger when team members become stakeholders who take personal pride in the outcome of the project. Consider the following five ways to help create a sense of project ownership: 1) Clearly define roles and responsibilities; 2) Ensure the organizational model supports accountability; 3) Tie incentives to success; 4) Foster communication throughout the organization; and 5) Obtain commitment from project participants. Preparation is key in establishing ownership. The roles of each member must be known to each other. Responsibility is making everyone accountable for their area of tasks and expertise.

Wired to Care: How Companies Prosper When They Create Widespread Empathy (FT Press, 2009) by Dev Patnaik offers help for being more passionate. The focus of the book is to enlighten organizations on how to be more empathic to their clients, employees, and stakeholders. The author reasons that organizations that have empathy are more successful, and presents several cases including Harley Davidson, Cisco, and Nike. For the project sponsor and manager such empathy is certainly required for a successful project. This suggests that successful project sponsors and managers must learn about their customers and passionately interact with them.

On Sunday morning, August 6, 1945, at 8:15 a.m. local time, the B-29 bomber Enola Gay dropped a uranium-fueled atomic bomb, Little Boy, on Hiroshima. On August 9, Nagasaki was devastated using a plutonium implosion-type atomic bomb, Fat Man, dropped by another B-29 bomber. Truman's decision argued that, given the tenacious Japanese defense of the outlying islands, the bombings saved hundreds of thousands of American lives that would have been lost in an invasion of mainland Japan. Truman himself wrote later in life that, "I knew what I was doing when I stopped the war. I have no regrets and, under the same circumstances, I would do it again." Truman passionately owned his decisions.

The Dead Presidents' Guide to Project Management

"Leadership is the art of getting someone else to do something you want done because he wants to do it."

Dwight David Eisenhower

Dwight D. Eisenhower was the 34th president of the United States from 1953 to 1961. Eisenhower graduated from West Point and his non-governmental occupation was a soldier. Before holding the office of president he held no governmental offices. Eisenhower served for a short time as the president of Columbia University. He was a career military man and rose to chief of staff of the Army. His significant accomplishment prior to becoming president was defeating Nazi Germany through the planning and execution of the D-Day campaign. His major presidential accomplishment was the development of the Interstate Highway System, which accelerated commercial growth and personal mobility. Eisenhower's lesson for project managers and executive sponsors is planning is everything; the plan itself is nothing.

A project plan is a formal, approved document used to guide both project execution and project control. The primary uses of the project plan are to document planning assumptions and decisions; facilitate communication among stakeholders; and document approved scope, cost, and schedule baselines. A project plan may be a summary or a detailed document. Eisenhower's plan was well thought out and well articulated to all parties involved. Eisenhower championed and communicated the importance of the plan to his leadership and stakeholders. He communicated parts of the plan to each organization and delineated their roles and responsibilities.

Four things Eisenhower would have had to do to create a plan are: 1) Establish a formal project plan with stepping-stones, tasks, resources, skills, and timelines. Make sure that all stakeholders have an understanding of what is expected for each one; 2) Develop metrics to enable you to measure and monitor the progress of the project; 3) Create a formal change management process with specific criteria for measuring the approval or rejection of changes; and 4) Build and maintain the structure of the project keeping the final goal in mind.

Eisenhower spelled out what problems each team's part solved, what the solution was, and how the solution would be accomplished. Eisenhower's plan was concise and to the point. A person could read, understand, digest, and repeat it. D-Day actually had two plans – the real plan and the fake plan. The real plan started in 1943 under the command of Eisenhower. General Eisenhower created Supreme Headquarters, Allied Expeditionary Force (SHAEF) as his project management office to invade Normandy. General George Patton became the leader of the fake project to invade Pas de Calais. He also had a fake project office. Eisenhower amassed over a million men and their support equipment. He set up shelter and training facilities. He executed training for the assault using a very detailed plan.

A good or effective project manager knows how to organize and manage the details. This starts with the planning of a project. It also includes the execution of the detailed plan, the tracking of all the activities, the reviewing of stepping-stones and tasks, and the managing of requirements changes or functions to arrive at the final specified goal.

Eisenhower's fake plan was an innovative and masterstroke to fool the Germans who thirsted for secret information. The fake plan had Patton building fake housing. He built a massive fake air force out of plywood. He built thousands of fake tanks, jeeps, and trucks out of plywood. He also built thousands of fake landing craft. From the German spy and surveillance planes, the fake housing and equipment looked real. However, the greatest deception of all was the fake radio messages and communication that the German intelligence obtained. With the fake messages and the surveillance flights, the Germans thought this was the real invasion force and they strongly believed the real invasion would come at Pas de Calais, led by General Patton. They thought that Eisenhower's army was a diversion. Germany kept their main force in Pas de Calais and their reserve force in Normandy. One of Eisenhower's most famous quotes is, "Plans are nothing; planning is everything."

The Dead Presidents' Guide to Project Management

> "Those who dare to fail miserably can achieve greatly."

John Fitzgerald Kennedy

John F. Kennedy was the 35th president of the United States from 1961 to 1963. Kennedy graduated from Harvard College and his non-governmental occupation was an author and sailor. Before holding the office of president he was a member of U.S. House of Representatives and a U.S. senator. His significant accomplishment prior to becoming president was as a Naval war hero. For his heroism he was awarded the Purple Heart and Bronze Star. Kennedy was also awarded a Pulitzer Prize for his book *Profiles in Courage* (Cardinal, 1956). His major presidential accomplishment was his inspiration and vision to land a man on the moon. Kennedy's lesson for project managers and executive sponsors is to inspire greatness.

The central role of a president is to inspire and encourage the country to move forward. Kennedy inspired and encouraged the country. Decades after his death Kennedy's words and deeds still inspire people around the globe to achieve greatness. Similarly, the central role of a project sponsor is to inspire and encourage the project and the team to move forward to the ultimate project goals. Inspiration taps into the project team's creative minds and gets them to think positively about the project and its goals. Inspiration is infectious, and showing enthusiasm will inspire the project team.

Executive sponsors need to provide inspiration to the project team and stakeholders. You cannot be a good project sponsor or leader if you cannot inspire people. You can learn all the techniques and technology, but if you cannot inspire people you should consider refusing the project sponsor role. Project sponsors are in a position to influence and help move the team forward to the ultimate project goals. In order to inspire the project team, an executive sponsor needs to find out what will motivate them and go beyond just putting in the time. Project sponsors and managers have great influence. Kennedy was a great influencer and an inspirational speaker as well. The book *Influencer: The New Science of Leading Change* (McGraw-Hill Education; 2nd edition, May 2013) by Joseph Grenny, Kerry Patterson, David Maxfield, Ron McMillan, and Al Switzler, is a basic primer and provides a starter toolkit on how to influence others.

Influencing people is one of the most important skills for project managers and executive sponsors. The authors of *Influencer* provide stories about a few renowned individuals who demonstrate significant influencer behaviors and analyze why they were successful. The stories include an Indian bank specializing in micro loans, reducing AIDS in Thailand, eradicating the guinea worm, and an environment that changes criminal behavior.

Project sponsors need to continually inspire people all the way through to the end of the project. As a project sponsor, you just cannot rally the project team, leadership, and stakeholders at the beginning of the project and never go back to them until the end. The project sponsor has to continually inspire greatness. This is especially true when things go wrong or when there are delays in the project. Inspiration carries people through the rough times as well as the good times. Inspiration motivates the unmotivated and neutralizes the project saboteurs, detractors, and toxic members. Inspiration keeps people engaged in the project.

In 1961, Kennedy said the nation would put a man on the moon within a decade. It was a clear, simple, and great inspirational vision. In 1969, the United States landed a man on the moon, fulfilling Kennedy's simple vision. However, getting there was a different story – the space program was complex, with hundreds of projects. But the greatest thing Kennedy's vision did was to put everyone at NASA on the same page, without any ambiguity. A clear and simple vision statement coming from the executive sponsor is a leading precondition for project success. Of course, like most things in life, this is easier said than done.

The Dead Presidents' Guide to Project Management

> "You aren't learning anything
> when you're talking."

Lyndon Baines Johnson

Lyndon B. Johnson was the 36th president of the United States from 1963 to 1969. Johnson graduated from Texas State University and his non-governmental occupation was a teacher. Before holding the office of president he was a member of the U.S. House of Representatives, a U.S. senator, and vice president under John F. Kennedy. His significant accomplishment prior to becoming president was as the catalyst for the creation of the National Aeronautics and Space Administration (NASA), passage of the Civil Rights Act of 1964, and many other legislative achievements. His major presidential accomplishment was the "Great Society," otherwise known as the Economic Opportunity Act. Johnson's lesson for project managers and executive sponsors is to prevent fraudulence.

The Standish Group defines fraudulence as an action intended to deceive; it is deliberate trickery intended to gain an advantage or to avoid confrontation. Fraudulence can take many forms. In our book *The Public Execution of Miss Scarlet*, the title character does many things to try to cover up the real status of the project. Some of the things she does are intended to deceive her superiors and co-workers by offering false hope. Other things she does only fool herself into believing that she can turn things around.

There are four things an organization can do to combat fraudulence: 1) Mandate that all personnel in the organization attend ethics training and educational programs; 2) Have a system that can be seen from all angles and by all stakeholders. This will create an open and honest environment; 3) Use a standard measurement for tracking progress. Be sure to make it easy and understandable; and 4) Have a formal change process that will prevent blindsiding and show the impact of changes on requirements.

The Johnson administration did not follow these steps. In the mid-1960s, as part of Johnson's "Great Society," the United States Congress passed the Economic Opportunity Act. This act, part of Johnson's "War on Poverty," provided employers with incentives, through grants and advanced payments, to train the very poor, which was considered to be any person who had been unemployed for more than 18 months, or made less than $3,000 per year. Employers waved money at anyone (including drug addicts, ex-convicts, and the homeless) they could drag in off the streets. In Washington, D.C., the heroin community learned all they had to do was sign up for a training program, stay long enough to get paid, and then leave and get a fix. According to a post-audit finding, it turned out that half the enrollments in Washington, D.C., were drug addicts.

In our book, Miss Scarlet found herself in a similar web of lies with no way to get out. She finally comes clean and confronts her superiors and the corporate leadership on the real status of the project. They do not believe her. Her stakeholders also refuse to believe the project is going badly. She does convince them that she cooked the books. The leadership brings in an outside consultant to get the project back on track.

Unlike Miss Scarlet's superiors, employers that were training drug addicts, ex-convicts, and the homeless were not fooling anyone. The Washington bureaucrats knew what was going on and, at first, reported up the line. The response that came back was a request for higher enrollments. When they could not get higher enrollments the bureaucrats fudged the numbers. This practice was widely known all the way up to Johnson. Johnson's rationale was that his problem was not with the implementation, but with Congress. He wanted Congress to believe things were working and he would later fix the implementation. For if Congress knew that the programs were not effective, it would cut them out of the budget and the program would be lost. Therefore, Johnson cooked the books. Nixon killed the program when he was elected in 1968. Johnson's Great Society program failed because of fraudulence.

The Dead Presidents' Guide to Project Management

> "A man is not finished
> when he's defeated. He's finished
> when he quits."

Richard Milhous Nixon

Richard M. Nixon was the 37th president of the United States from 1969 to 1974. Nixon graduated from Whittier College and Duke University Law School and his non-governmental occupation was a lawyer. Nixon served in the Navy during World War II. Before holding the office of president he was a member of the U.S. House of Representatives, a U.S. senator, and vice president under Eisenhower. His significant accomplishment prior to becoming president was managing the House Un-American Activities Committee. His major presidential accomplishment was ending the Vietnam War. Nixon's lesson for project managers and executive sponsors is that too much arrogance is not a good idea.

Arrogance is the unwarranted, overbearing pride evidenced by a superior manner toward superiors, peers, and inferiors. Arrogance correlates pretty closely with past successes. Very often you will run into a development team that just completed a successful project, and they are so full of themselves that they fall prey to "overambition" and think they are infallible. Arrogance also correlates with intelligence and creativity. The line between confidence and arrogance is very blurry. It is very important for executive sponsors and project managers to know when a person has crossed the line from self-confidence into arrogance. Often people will go from confidence to arrogance without realizing it.

In recent Standish Group research, CIOs rated their project workforce as not very skilled at dealing with arrogance. One CIO said the best way to deal with arrogance is to know two things: who are your allies, and who are *not* your allies. Nixon thought the same thing and created an enemies list, and then used the power of the presidency to persecute the people on the list. He would order the FBI, CIA, and the IRS to go after his opponents. Nixon went from confident to insecure to arrogant without realizing it.

Nixon is not unique. In their book *What Got You Here Won't Get You There: How Successful People Become Even More Successful* (Hachette Books, January 2007), Marshall Goldsmith and Mark Reiter outline 20 bad habits that sink most up-and-coming executives. However, these bad habits can be summed up in one word: arrogance. Consider this scenario described by Pauline Nist, GM for Enterprise Software Strategy at Intel Corp. She had a very brilliant but corrosive engineer on a server project team. When other engineers on the team put their specs online for comment and feedback this engineer would insult them and belittle their ideas online – but never face-to-face. After a while the whole environment became hostile. Like Nixon, he was arrogant and he was removed from the team for the good of the project.

To deal with arrogance you must confront it directly. If the group itself is arrogant, then do exercises on all the potential project risks. This exercise tends to cool down arrogance. If it is an individual, then you can try to learn from the person's experience and feed his or her ego while attempting to mitigate the person's negative effect on others and the project. If you tie advancement and compensation to the success of a project, it will tend to get people to work together better. Building consensus within an arrogant environment is a difficult task, but must be accomplished in order for the project to succeed. Contingency planning can take the starch out of the most arrogant person.

The Watergate scandal is another good example of how Nixon crossed the line from self-confidence into arrogance. The Watergate scandal was caused by five men linked to the committee to re-elect the president when they were caught breaking into the Democratic Party's headquarters at the Watergate complex in Washington, D.C., on June 17, 1972. It became clear that Nixon's aides had committed the crime in an attempt to sabotage the Democrats in their bid to take back the White House. Nixon arrogantly tried to cover it up rather than admit the transgression. He is the only president to resign from office.

The Dead Presidents' Guide to Project Management

"When a man is asked to make a speech,
the first thing he has to decide is what to say."

Gerald Rudolph Ford

Gerald R. Ford was the 38th president of the United States from 1974 to 1977. Ford graduated from the University of Michigan and Yale University Law School. At Michigan, Ford was a star linebacker and was offered tryouts by both the Green Bay Packers and the Detroit Lions. His non-governmental occupation was a lawyer. Before holding the office of president he was a member of the U.S. House of Representatives and vice president under Richard Nixon. His significant accomplishment prior to becoming president was serving as House minority leader. His major presidential accomplishment was healer of the nation and gaining the trust of the people after the Watergate Scandal. His lesson for project managers and executive sponsors is to get the chemistry right.

Chemistry is hard to define, never mind manage. It is one of those things that you know when you have it, and it's painfully obvious when you do not have it. We have all seen enough TV programs and movies to recognize good and bad chemistry. Some actors just work better together. The same is true with project team members. Building and maintaining team chemistry is an ongoing process, which should include participation from the team. Each member needs to clearly know his or her roles and responsibilities. The staff needs to be properly motivated and have the proper skill set.

The culture of the organization is a key factor in team chemistry. If a team member or members are not aligned with the general organizational culture they may have problems working together. A major problem IT departments must contend with during a corporate consolidation is how to maintain the staff chemistry. Common interest sets the stage for good chemistry. Human nature appears to be such that we take much better care of people who are like us.

Ford had good chemistry with others. People generally liked him and thought of him as a good and caring person. He was a good teammate on the football team. He was a good Navy leader and performed well under fire. He was a good congressman, serving in the House of Representatives from 1949 to 1973. He was well liked on all sides of the political spectrum. He rose to minority leader because people trusted him. When Spiro Agnew resigned as vice president in the wake of a scandal, Nixon named Ford to replace him. Nixon was in the middle of his own Watergate scandal and had little political capital to get a more prominent vice president. Ford was considered safe and would not compete with other rivals for president. He was confirmed easily with 387 votes for and 35 against.

In contrast to Ford, Nixon had bad chemistry. As we have learned, good chemistry can produce extraordinary results, while bad chemistry can create conflicts. There are four ways a project sponsor or manager can create good chemistry and resolve conflicts: 1) Pay close attention to how team members interact. Watch for telltale signs of a brewing conflict: glaring stares, crossed arms, clenched fists, sarcasm; 2) Arrange for early team training in conflict management; 3) Toss the problem onto the middle of the table. This proven technique works when the team leader openly and without bias invites the participating members to contribute to a compromise; and 4) Lay down the ground rules.

When Ford took over the presidency in 1974 from the disgraced Nixon the country was full of raw wounds. Ford's first step was to pardon Nixon in order to start healing the nation. Then he pardoned Vietnam War draft evaders, again to help heal the nation. Then he went on to fix a difficult economy and runaway inflation, which soothed a troubled nation, and he enjoyed a good relationship with the citizens. However, he never won their respect and was often the butt of jokes. While Ford lost the election for his only bid for the presidency, he did make the chemistry of the country better.

The Dead Presidents' Guide to Project Management

"Trust, but verify."

Ronald Wilson Reagan

Ronald Reagan was the 40th president of the United States from 1981 to 1989. Reagan graduated from Eureka College and his non-governmental occupation was an actor, plus TV and radio announcer. As an actor he made several films including *Hellcats of the Navy* (1957) and *Knute Rockne, All American* (1940). Before holding the office of president he was governor of California and president of the Screen Actors Guild. His significant accomplishment prior to becoming president was the creation of the actor's residual payment system. His major presidential accomplishment was ending the Cold War. Reagan is considered "the great communicator" and his lesson for project managers and executive sponsors is to be a good communicator.

Reagan developed a habit of communicating just the right amount of information to get his message across. Through his years of acting and public service Reagan developed a keen sense of how and how much information to deliver so the information was both clear and understandable, and so it would be retained by the listener. For example, Reagan said: "There are no constraints on the human mind, no walls around the human spirit, and no barriers to our progress except those we ourselves erect." A good communicator knows the difference between too little information and too much information.

Good communication requires speaking to the listeners in their language and customs and listening to what they have to say. The project sponsor and manager must understand the organization enough to communicate effectively with the project community. Good communicators refrain from using too much technical jargon and focus on the business elements so communication is clearly understood. The project team should be proactive in soliciting stakeholders' opinions especially around business functions and requirements. Good communication is demonstrated through both acts and deeds, not just words.

Reagan's greatest talent was setting the agenda and communicating his vision. Much of his agenda was based on his personal beliefs. Reagan surrounded himself with the best people he could find. He would delegate his authority and not interfere with his people as long as his policies were being carried out. In this regard he would rally both his staff and followers around these beliefs and get them to believe that they were their beliefs as well. This phenomenon became known as the Reagan Revolution. While this part of the job is the executive sponsor's function, project professionals need to help and guide the project sponsor. The seasoned project manager learns how much information to present and how much information not to present. Information overload is as much a threat to objectivity and transparency as too little information.

Reagan was not a natural good communicator. He worked at it. He selected opportunities to work on his communication skills. These opportunities included radio commercials and TV talk shows, Hollywood movies, television programs and commercials, and stage. He believed that a lot of the trouble in the world would disappear if we were talking to each other instead of about each other.

A good example of Reagan's communication abilities was during his first presidential campaign. Winning the New Hampshire Primary is considered a gateway to the presidency. In 1980, Ronald Reagan paid to host a Republican debate in Nashua, New Hampshire. The debate was to be between only the two front-running candidates, George H. Bush and Ronald Reagan. Reagan invited the other candidates at the last minute. However, George Bush refused to go on with the debate with the other candidates. On the stage, Bush and Reagan sat on high stools and the moderator started the debate when the other five candidates walked in the room behind Bush and Reagan. Reagan started to explain into the microphone why the other candidates would not be joining them when the moderator, Jon Breen, cut him off. At that point, using good communication and a show of leadership, Reagan got up off the stool and said, "I am paying for this microphone, Mr. Green [Breen]."

The Dead Presidents' Guide to Project Management

"Be bold in your dreaming"

George H. W. Bush

George H. W. Bush was the 41st president of the United States from 1989 to 1993. Bush graduated from Yale University and began his career as an executive in the oil and gas industry. Before holding the office of president, he was a member of the U.S. House of Representatives, after which he served as the U.S. Ambassador to the United Nations, the Director of the Central Intelligence Agency, and finally Vice President, under Ronald Reagan. Bush also served as a Navy Avenger bomber pilot in World War Two. He flew 58 combat missions, was shot down once, and received the Distinguished Flying Cross and three Air Medals. Bush was a model of civility and decorum. His lesson for project managers and executive sponsors is to keep projects small and to make firm, quick decisions.

The Standish Group has determined that the root cause of software project failures and challenges is slow decision latency. Decision latency theory states: "The value of the interval is greater than the quality of the decision." Therefore, to improve project performance, organizations need to consider ways to speed up their decisions. This is outlined in detail in our CHAOS Report on Decision Latency Theory (2018). George H. W. Bush's flying experience taught him the value of making quick decisions and to always keep moving forward. His years in the oil exploitation industry taught him that decisions can be risky, but Bush did not shy away from making them. He learned to own his decisions, and if things did not work out, he was prepared to accept the responsibility for the consequences.

In our book, *The Good Mate: How understanding team relationships can make you happier and more productive* (2019), Evan Sorensen and I outline 50 basic skills you can use to improve being a good teammate. By understanding and improving on these basic skills, you can in fact be the beacon who helps your teammates. You do this not by direction or mandates; you do it by being a good example. You do it by being a good mate. George H. W. Bush was a great teammate. He embodied many of the principles we invoke, especially those that involve being influential, civil, and respectful. These skills were never more evident than in the manner with which Bush conducted himself during his vice presidency under Ronald Reagan. He didn't shy away from being influential with the president, but he never openly aired their differences.

George H. W. Bush was a great listener. The art of listening, of course, is one of the most important skills that any person can develop. Bush learned very early in life that listening offered him a better understanding of another person's point of view. In fact, he went out of his way to search out colleagues with different viewpoints. During his presidency he often went to the Congressional Gym, finding it a good place to strike up casual conversation with both Republicans and Democrats. He was good at reflecting back a speaker's words to confirm his understanding, and would listen with empathy. (Empathy is another good teammate skill.) In fact, Bush has been quoted as saying, *"Don't confuse being 'soft' with seeing the other guy's point of view."*

The Standish Group has proven time and time again that there is a direct correlation between the size and complexity of a project and its chances of a successful resolution and high-value outcome. The larger the project and the greater its complexity, the higher the risk of failure. Conversely, the smaller the project and the easier its goals, the higher the success rate. This is true no matter how you measure success.

The Standish Group has defined six Success options and modifications: 1) OnTime; 2) OnBudget; 3) OnTarget; 4) Customer Satisfaction with Very Satisfied, Satisfied, and Somewhat Satisfied ranges; 5) Return of Value with Very High, High, and Average Value ranges; and 6) Goal of [??] the corporate strategy with Precise, Close, and Loose ranges. Using each of these separately or in any combination will bear out this fact.

On August 2, 1990, Iraq invaded and annexed Kuwait, leaving it an occupied country for more than six months. During this six-month interval, George H. W. Bush unsuccessfully negotiated with Iraq to leave Kuwait and return that country to the status of an independent sovereign nation. Failing to negotiate a peaceful settlement, Bush created a coalition of a 40-nation military force with a clear vision to drive Iraq out of Kuwait. On January 17, 1991, Bush launched Operation Desert Storm, and within 100 hours, Iraq was driven out of Kuwait. The international coalition would remain together for another six weeks to reduce Iraq's ability to reinvade Kuwait. George H. W. Bush purposely kept the project small and straightforward, with clearly defined goals and objectives.

Summary

Forty presidents and 40 lessons, from George Washington to George H. W. Bush. We learned from failure and how to be a good communicator. We learned about inspiring people. We learned about ignorance, arrogance, overambition, abstinence, and fraudulence. We learned less is more, but not to forget the big picture. We learned a lot about communication, such as when there is too much or too little, having a good communication platform, listening, being visible, and using social media. We learned how to deal with a toxic team member, the project saboteur, and getting the chemistry right. We learned about emotional maturity and how important it is to project success.

We also learned about good habits such as making timely decisions, making connections, and collaborating. We learned about planning, ownership, and creating a project community. We learned about some common agile techniques such as iteration, stepping-stones, and innovations. We learned about being a good mentor. We learned about process, risk, and failure tolerance. We learned about setting expectations, managing trade-offs, and focusing on real user needs. We learned from these 40 men about gaining consensus and feedback. We learned from these men how to be good project managers and good executive sponsors.

Sources

The majority of the *Dead Presidents' Guide to Project Management* was plagiarized. However, the plagiarism is from my own writings in the *CHAOS Reports*, *CHAOS Knowledge Center*, *PM2GO.com*, *Café CHAOS*, *CHAOS Newsletters*, skills assessments, and other published material under my authorship. Much of what was taken was clipped, edited, and changed to fit the story.

The original presidential stories were created from my personal dead presidential library. A full list of the books can be found on www.standishgroup.com/potus.

Certain facts, quotes, and verifications came from potus.com, Brainyquote.com, and other general Internet searches. Many of the ideas and thought leadership for project executive sponsors came from the Executive Sponsor Research Report and the executive sponsor interview series.

I thank the following executives for participating in these interviews:
- Lon Allan: corporate lawyer in Silicon Valley
- Dave Bealby: international management consultant and venture angel
- Gene Bounds: senior executive in project management services
- Timothy Chou: author, teacher, and senior technology executive
- Bill Coleman: partner with the venture capital firm Alsop Louie
- Larry Fleming: senior IT executive
- Don Haderle: IBM Fellow, CTO, and the father of DB2
- Ellen Hancock: experienced CEO and board member
- Bill Heil: senor technology and marketing executive

Executive Sponsor Interview participants continued:

- George Hogan: CIO and senior executive
- B. Lee Jones: experienced and seasoned CIO
- Robert Kelley: CIO and senior IT professional
- Shahin Khan: senior technology and marketing executive
- Jim Kneeland: CIO and project management executive
- Daniel Langermann: senior management consultant
- Gloria Cordes Larson: government, academia, and private senior executive
- Mike Nemerowski: CEO, CTO, and CIO
- Eric Newcomer: CTO and technology consultant
- Bill Niemi: CTO and technology consultant
- Pauline Nist: professional systems general manager
- David Saul: senior executive and scientist of technology
- Mike Sledge: senior executive for project management services
- Richard Soley: senior executive for standards and industry consortiums
- Albert Soule: senior executive for project management services
- Jeff Sutherland: principal co-founder of Scrum
- Bob Taylor: professional CTO
- Kirby Wadsworth: chief marketing officer

The Dead Presidents' Guide to Project Management

"Time is the enemy of all projects."

About the Author

Jim Johnson is a professor at the Antwerp Management Schools and Chief Dreamer of The Standish Group. He has been professionally involved in the computer industry for over 50 years and has a long list of published books, papers, articles and speeches. He has a combination of technical, marketing and research achievements focused on mission-critical applications and technology. He is best known for his research on project performance and early recognition and predictions of emerging technology trends. Jim is a pioneer of modern research techniques and continues to advance study methodologies in the research industry through case-based analytical technology.

Other books by Jim Johnson include:
CHAOS Report: Decision Latency Theory: It's All About the Interval
The Good Mate
The Good Sponsor
Executive Doodle Book
My Life is Failure
The Public Execution of Miss Scarlet
Executive Sponsor Research Report
Emotional Maturity Research Report
20 years of CHAOS Reports

Children's Books
Dragon2Dragon
Saving Jimmy: Adventures of Jackie the Squirrel

www.ingramcontent.com/pod-product-compliance
Lightning Source LLC
Chambersburg PA
CBHW021233090426
42740CB00006B/518